The U.S. Freedom of Information Act at 50

The federal Freedom of Information Act, which recently turned 50, has been hailed as the primary means by which U.S. citizens can know about how their governors operate in a democratic republic. Recently, however, it has been criticized as ineffective because it is cumbersome and full of loopholes. This book examines the role and effectiveness of the FOIA (Freedom of Information Act), comparing the FOIA world with the pre-FOIA world, rating its effectiveness compared to other access laws internationally, examining ways in which it can be improved, and questioning whether it should be dismantled and replaced.

This book was originally published as a special issue of *Communication Law and Policy.*

W. Wat Hopkins is a Professor of Communication at Virginia Tech University, US. He teaches and writes about free speech, is the editor of a textbook on communication law, and is editor of the scholarly journal *Communication Law and Policy.*

The U.S. Freedom of Information Act at 50

Edited by
W. Wat Hopkins

Routledge
Taylor & Francis Group
LONDON AND NEW YORK

First published 2018
by Routledge

2 Park Square, Milton Park, Abingdon, Oxfordshire OX14 4RN
52 Vanderbilt Avenue, New York, NY 10017

Routledge is an imprint of the Taylor & Francis Group, an informa business

First issued in paperback 2020

British Library Cataloguing-in-Publication Data
A catalogue record for this book is available from the British Library

ISBN13: 978-1-138-57608-7 (hbk)
ISBN13: 978-0-367-53004-4 (pbk)

Typeset in Minion Pro
by codeMantra

Publisher's Note
The publisher accepts responsibility for any inconsistencies that may have arisen during the conversion of this book from journal articles to book chapters, namely the possible inclusion of journal terminology.

Disclaimer
Every effort has been made to contact copyright holders for their permission to reprint material in this book. The publishers would be grateful to hear from any copyright holder who is not here acknowledged and will undertake to rectify any errors or omissions in future editions of this book.

Contents

Citation Information

The chapters in this book were originally published in *Communication Law and Policy*, volume 21, issue 4 (Autumn 2016). When citing this material, please use the original page numbering for each article, as follows:

Introduction
W. Wat Hopkins
Communication Law and Policy, volume 21, issue 4 (Autumn 2016) pp. 431–432

Chapter 1
The People's Right to Know: Comparing Harold L. Cross' Pre-FOIA World to Post-FOIA Today
David Cuillier
Communication Law and Policy, volume 21, issue 4 (Autumn 2016) pp. 433–463

Chapter 2
The Fiftieth Anniversary of the Freedom of Information Act: How it Measures up Against International Standards and Other Laws
Toby Mendel
Communication Law and Policy, volume 21, issue 4 (Autumn 2016) pp. 465–491

Chapter 3
The News Media and the FOIA
Derigan Silver
Communication Law and Policy, volume 21, issue 4 (Autumn 2016) pp. 493–514

Chapter 4
Bringing Back Full Disclosure: A Call for Dismantling FOIA
Daxton R. "Chip" Stewart and Charles N. Davis
Communication Law and Policy, volume 21, issue 4 (Autumn 2016) pp. 515–537

Chapter 5
Controlling Discourse, Foreclosing Recourse: The Creep of the Glomar Response
A. Jay Wagner
Communication Law and Policy, volume 21, issue 4 (Autumn 2016) pp. 539–567

For any permission-related enquiries please visit:
http://www.tandfonline.com/page/help/permissions

Notes on Contributors

David Cuillier is Associate Professor and Director of the School of Journalism at the University of Arizona, US. He is the editor of *Transparency 2.0: Digital Data and Privacy in a Wired World* (with Charles N. Davis, 2014).

Charles N. Davis is Professor and Dean of the College of Journalism and Mass Communication at the University of Georgia, US. He is the author of *Principles of American Journalism* (with Stephanie Craft, 2013) and editor of *Transparency 2.0: Digital data and privacy in a wired world* (with David Cuillier, 2014).

W. Wat Hopkins is a Professor of Communication at Virginia Tech University, US. He teaches and writes about free speech, is the editor of a textbook on communication law, and is editor of the scholarly journal *Communication Law and Policy.*

Toby Mendel is Executive Director and President of the Centre for Law and Democracy, based in Halifax, Canada. He has published extensively on a range of topics, such as freedom of expression; right to information; communication rights; and refugee issues, including comparative legal and analytical studies on public service broadcasting, the right to information, and broadcast policy.

Derigan Silver is Associate Professor in the Department of Media, Film and Journalism Studies at the University of Denver, US. He teaches on the First Amendment, media law, and Internet law, and is the author of several articles and book chapters on access to government information.

Daxton R. "Chip" Stewart is Associate Professor and Dean of the College of Communication at Texas Christian University, US. His areas of expertise include media law and communication technology, the First Amendment, freedom of information and public records laws, and social media.

A. Jay Wagner is Assistant Professor in the College of Communications and Fine Arts, Bradley University, Illinois, US. His research focuses on access to government information, in particular the Freedom of Information Act and populous transparency movements.

INTRODUCTION

The First Amendment might be the single most definitive indicator of the type of democratic republic established in the years following the American Revolution. Key to the proper working of that democratic republic is the notion that speech of self-governing importance is most effective when the populace has access to information about how governing occurs. That's why the federal Freedom of Information Act, which turns fifty this year, is important.

This special issue of *Communication Law and Policy* celebrates that birthday in an important way: It provides background and analysis of how well FOIA is working, and suggestions for how it could work better.

The idea for the issue is that of David Cuillier, Director of the School of Journalism at the University of Arizona, and one of the country's leading access advocates. David and some of his colleagues suggested a list of topics that might be covered and authors who could write about those topics, and, after some discussion, a lineup for the issue was established. The authors who were invited to write, without exception, accepted the invitations.

As a result, this issue contains five exceptional articles.[1]

David Cuillier examines how access has changed between 1953, when Harold L. Cross wrote *The People's Right to Know,* and today. He uses Cross' analysis of access in the mid-twentieth century to recommend changes to make FOIA better.

Toby Mendel, Director of the Centre for Law and Democracy in Canada, delineates exactly why the federal FOIA does not stand up to international scrutiny. Among nations with similar laws, ours ranks fifty-second, and does not provide the access guarantees it promised fifty years ago.

Professor Derigan Silver explores the use of FOIA by representatives of the news media, and provides suggestions as to how changes in both

[1]The article by A.Jay Wagner was submitted by the author and went through the regular selection process, that is, it was accepted after peer-review. The other articles were invited by the editor and Professor Cuillier.

the law and the procedures used by journalists can improve the information flow to the general public.

Professors Daxton R. "Chip" Stewart and Charles N. Davis propose a solution for the failures of FOIA to accomplish the goals promised by its adoption. Rather than providing a presumption of openness, they write, under FOIA documents are presumed to be closed until a request for access is made. They propose a three-part scheme for using technology to provide the fullest possible disclosure of agency records.

Professor A.Jay Wagner writes about the expanded use of the so-called "Glomar response" to requests for records under FOIA. The response – which was designed for rare occasions when even the acknowledgement that a record on a national security topic exists – has grown from its original intent, Professor Wagner writes, so that it is now improperly used by state agencies, reducing government transparency.

The case made by all these articles is that FOIA is not doing the job that was intended, and that a major overhaul of the act is needed to ensure requisite access to government documents and activities. Access is key to a democratic republic, and fifty years after its adoption, FOIA must be revised to provide that access.

THE PEOPLE'S RIGHT TO KNOW: COMPARING HAROLD L. CROSS' PRE-FOIA WORLD TO POST-FOIA TODAY

DAVID CUILLIER

Journalists and politicians often disagree over whether the state of freedom of information is better or worse since the passage of the Freedom of Information Act in 1966. This study attempts to provide some historical context by comparing the state of access in 1953 as outlined in detail in The People's Right to Know *by Harold L. Cross, the first comprehensive review of case law and statutes in the United States regarding access to public records at local, state and federal agencies. Analysis indicates that the legal right to information, particularly for police records and federal documents, is better today than it was in 1953, but challenges persist regarding compliance, enforcement and the prevalence of exemptions. Recommendations are provided for the next fifty years, including renewal of Cross' urging for a First Amendment right to know.*

> "Public business is the public's business. The people have a right to know. Freedom of information is their just heritage. Without that the citizens of a democracy have but changed their kings."[1]

These words opened the 1953 book by Harold L. Cross that fueled the twentieth century transparency movement in the United States[2]

---

[1]HAROLD L. CROSS, THE PEOPLE'S RIGHT TO KNOW: LEGAL ACCESS TO PUBLIC RECORDS AND PROCEEDINGS xiii (1953).

[2]*See* HERBERT N. FOERSTEL, FREEDOM OF INFORMATION AND THE RIGHT TO KNOW: THE ORIGINS AND APPLICATIONS OF THE FREEDOM OF INFORMATION ACT 17 (1999) (noting that Cross' systematic assessment of government policies and practices confirmed journalists' feelings that secrecy inhibited information getting to the public); SHANNON E. MARTIN, FREEDOM OF INFORMATION: THE NEWS THE MEDIA USE 52 (2008) (writing that "[m]uch of the text is a legal roadmap to case law and statutes that guided the discourse on public records and 'a right to know' about government activities"); MICHAEL SCHUDSON THE RISE OF THE RIGHT TO KNOW: POLITICS AND THE CULTURE OF TRANSPARENCY,

and "became the Bible of the press and ultimately a roadmap for the Congress regarding freedom of information."[3] In the more than six decades since the publication of Cross' book, citizen access to government documents has been codified through the federal Freedom of Information Act,[4] enshrined in dozens of states through modernized public record laws, and interpreted by state and federal courts. The United States is regarded as a world leader in freedom of information,[5] and the legal right to access government documents is touted as fundamental to democracy,[6] and essential for the press' ability to provide citizens the information they need to self-govern.[7]

Journalists and public officials, however, disagree over whether freedom of information is actually better today than in the past. President Barack Obama declared his administration the most transparent in the nation's history,[8] yet, journalists say the Obama administration has

1945-1975, 42 (2016) (referring to the work as "the much-cited bible of the freedom-of-information movement"); Sam Archibald, *The Early Years of the Freedom of Information Act – 1955 to 1974,* 26 POL. SCI. & POL. 727 (1993) (writing that Cross' book highlighted the fact that federal laws were being co-opted as tools of secrecy); Bernard Botein, *Book Notes,* 67 HARV. L. REV. 920 (1954) (calling the work "an excellent handbook which is an essential for editors and which will be useful to lawyers").

[3]MICHAEL R. LEMOV, PEOPLE'S WARRIOR: JOHN MOSS AND THE FIGHT FOR FREEDOM OF INFORMATION AND CONSUMER RIGHTS 49 (2011).

[4]5 U.S.C. § 552 (2016).

[5]*See* David Banisar, *Freedom of Information Around the World 2006: A Global Survey of Access to Government Information Laws, in* PRIVACY INTERNATIONAL 5 (2006), *available at* http://www.freedominfo.org/documents/global_survey2006.pdf (last visited July 16, 2016) (explaining that while not the first FOIA law to be enacted in the world, the U.S. FOIA was a milestone that other countries have modeled).

[6]*See* ALEXANDER MEIKLEJOHN, FREE SPEECH AND ITS RELATION TO SELF-GOVERNMENT (1948) (arguing that access to information is essential for self-government); Vincent Blasi, *The Checking Value in First Amendment Theory,* 2 LAW & SOC. INQUIRY 521 (1977) (arguing that "the First Amendment may require that journalists have access as a general matter to some records").

[7]*See, e.g.,* Barbara A. Almanza, Joseph Ismail & Juline E. Mills, *The Impact of Publishing Foodservice Inspection Scores,* 5 J. FOODSERVICE BUS. RES. 45-62 (2002) (showing that publicized food safety inspections decrease consumer complaints); Lori S. Bennear & Sheila M. Olmstead, *The Impacts of the "Right to Know": Information Disclosure and the Violation of Drinking Water Standards,* 56 J. ENVTL. ECON. & MGMT. 117-30 (2008) (requiring disclosure of drinking water contaminants reduces health violations); Society of Professional Journalists, *Open Doors Survey* (2002), http://www.spj.org/opendoors5.asp (last visited July 13, 2016) (outlining the prevalence of public records in news stories based on a content-analysis of more than 3,000 stories). In addition, the Sunshine in Government Initiative's FOIA Files is a database of more than 700 news stories made possible through FOIA, http://sunshineingovernment.org/wordpress/the-foia-files/ (last visited July 13, 2016).

[8]Exec. Order No. 13,489, 36 C.F.R. 1270 (2009), *reprinted in* 44 U.S.C. § 2204 (2009). President Barack Obama signed an executive order and two memoranda his first day of office, Jan. 21, 2009, calling for a new era of openness. Exec. Order No. 13,489, 74 F.R. 4669 (Jan. 21, 2009) (Presidential Records), *available*

been the most secretive.[9] In 2015, the Society of Professional Journalists and fifty-two other journalism organizations sent a letter to the White House urging an end to excessive information controls by public information officers, "essentially forms of censorship – that have surged at all levels of government in the past few decades."[10] Investigative reporter Ted Gupp wrote in 2007: "Today America is a nation of secrets, an increasingly furtive land where closed doors outnumber open ones and where it is no longer 'the right to know' but 'the need to know' that is the measure against which access is determined."[11]

Access advocates also point to the relative weakness of U.S. FOIA, at least on paper, in relation to the more than 100 other countries that have adopted freedom of information laws. According to one

at http://www.whitehouse.gov/the-press-office/presidential-records; Exec. Order No. 13,490, 74 F.R. 4673 (Jan. 21, 2009) (Ethics Commitments by Executive Branch Personnel), *available at* http://www.whitehouse.gov/the-press-office/ethics-commitments-executive-branch-personnel (last visited July 16, 2016). Later the president would declare his administration the most transparent in U.S. history. *See* Jonathan Easley, *Obama Says his is "Most Transparent Administration" Ever,* THE HILL, Feb. 14, 2013, *available at* http://thehill.com/blogs/blog-briefing-room/news/283335-obama-this-is-the-most-transparent-administration-in-history (last visited July 18, 2016).

[9] *See* Jason Ross Arnold, *Has Obama Delivered the "Most Transparent" Administration in History?,* WASH. POST, Mar. 16, 2015, *available at* https://www.washingtonpost.com/blogs/monkey-cage/wp/2015/03/16/has-obama-delivered-the-most-transparent-administration-in-history/ (last visited July 16, 2016); Kenneth T. Walsh, *Reporters Say Obama White House "Most Secretive" Ever,* U.S. NEWS & WORLD REPORT, May 1, 2014, *available at* http://www.usnews.com/news/blogs/ken-walshs-washington/2014/05/01/reporters-say-obama-white-house-most-secretive-ever (last visited July 16, 2016) (survey of sixty-one White House correspondents by *Politico Magazine* found that 42% agreed Obama is the most secretive they've ever covered); Ted Bridis & Jack Gillum, *U.S. Government Sets Record for Failures to Find Files When Asked,* ASSOCIATED PRESS, Mar. 18, 2016, http://bigstory.ap.org/article/697e3523003049cdb0847ecf828afd62/us-govt-sets-record-failures-find-files-when-asked (study by the Associated Press showed that 77% of FOIA requests in 2015 resulted in blacked out files or no records); Dylan Byers, *Jill Abramson: "This is the Most Secretive White House I Have Ever Dealt With,"* POLITICO, Jan. 23, 2014, *available at* http://www.politico.com/blogs/media/2014/01/jill-abramson-this-is-the-most-secretive-white-house-i-have-ever-dealt-with-181742 (last visited July 18, 2016).

[10] *Letter to President Obama,* SOC'Y. PROF. JOURNALISTS, Aug. 10, 2015, *available at* http://spj.org/pdf/news/obama-letter-final-08102015.pdf (last visited July 16, 2016). This letter followed a similar one sent July 8, 2014, on behalf of thirty-eight journalism organizations. *See* http://www.spj.org/news.asp?ref=1253, (last visited July 16, 2016). In full disclosure, the author of this article was president of the Society of Professional Journalists at the time of the first letter, and SPJ Freedom of Information Committee chairman at the time of the second letter.

[11] TED GUPP, NATION OF SECRETS: THE THREAT TO DEMOCRACY AND THE AMERICAN WAY OF LIFE 9 (2007) (outlining the prevalence of efforts to thwart journalists' access to information). *Also see* Robert McClure, *SEJ Study Finds FOIA Little Used, Plagued by Delays,* 15 SEJ J. 5 (2005) (interviews of fifty-five environmental journalists indicated that two-thirds didn't use FOIA because of perceptions that it does not work).

international assessment, U.S. FOIA's provisions place the strength of the law at fifty-first in the world, below, among others, Mexico, Russia and Kyrgyzstan.[12] In some parts of the globe, unlike in the United States, the right to know is not just a statutory right but also a constitutional right,[13] and in some cases, a fundamental human right.[14]

This disconnect begs the question: Since passage of FOIA in 1966 and its subsequent amendments, including those in 2016,[15] as well as the adoption of modern state public record laws, do citizens and the press have more or less access to government information? Are citizens better or worse off than they were before Congress enacted FOIA fifty years ago?

Some argue that passage of a law is irrelevant, and that statutes have little causal effect on the actual ability for a citizen or journalist to acquire government information; that the mood of the citizenry and times dictate cultural norms and practices; and that transparency and secrecy ebb and flow depending on societal forces, such as war and attitudes toward privacy.[16] Michael Schudson suggests a change in culture occurred between 1960 and 1980 in the United States toward

[12] Access Info Europe and the Centre for Law and Democracy rated 105 nations' FOIA laws by various categories for their Global Right to Information Rating, placing the U.S. FOIA at fifty-first in the world, https://www.rti-rating.org/country-data (last visited Aug. 8, 2016). While the ratings assess provisions in the law, they do not account for actual implementation.

[13] Some nations that recognize access to government information as a constitutional right are Argentina, Brazil, Colombia, El Salvador, Finland, Guatemala, Indonesia, Mexico, South Africa, South Sudan and Uganda. For a breakdown of all national FOIA laws in the world, *see* the Global Right to Information Rating by Access Info Europe and the Centre for Law and Democracy, *supra* note 12. *See also* Toby Mendel, *Freedom of Information: A Comparative Legal Survey* 20-21, 43-126 (2008), http://portal.unesco.org/ci/en/files/26159/12054862803freedom_information_en.pdf/freedom_information_en.pdf (last visited July 16, 2016).

[14] *See* Cheryl Ann Bishop, Access to Information as a Human Right 21-24 (2012) (explaining the legal reasoning international courts have put forth to determine that access to government information is a human right).

[15] FOIA Improvement Act of 2016, Pub. L. No. 114-185 (2016) (provisions include codifying the presumption of openness, greater independence for the Office of Government Information Services, and mandate for a single online FOIA portal for requesters).

[16] *See* Jeannine E. Relly & Meghna Sabharwal, *Perceptions of Transparency of Government Policymaking: A Cross-National Study,* 26 Gov't. Info. Q. 155 (2009) (An analysis of nations' FOIA laws indicates that democratic governance has little to do with actual transparency and that many FOIA laws may be merely cosmetic.); Barry Sullivan, *FOIA and the First Amendment: Representative Democracy and the People's Elusive "Right to Know,"* 72 Md. L. Rev. 6 (2012) (writing, "The extent to which government recognizes the right of access to information depends on society's view of citizenship and on the strength of its commitment to that view").

information openness, a shift in opinion, beliefs and "structures of feeling," which led to creation of FOIA laws – not caused by the laws.[17]

David Banisar points out that despite the flood of FOIA laws enacted around the world in the early 2000s:

> The culture of secrecy remains strong in many countries. Many of the laws are not adequate and promote access in name only. In some countries, the laws lie dormant due to a failure to implement them properly or a lack of demand. In others, the exemptions and fees are abused by governments... New laws promoting secrecy in the global war on terror have undercut access.[18]

Some studies suggest that FOIA laws actually *hinder* access by providing public officials legal rationales for delays, excessive copy fees, and denial. For example, Lindita Camaj interviewed journalists in Kosovo regarding their experience in accessing information since the country adopted FOIA in 2003. Journalists reported that the law was little use to them because of long delays and that public officials co-opted the law to obstruct access, not facilitate it.[19]

Researchers are limited in their ability to compare the state of access before FOIA to the state of transparency today. Surveys of journalists and public officials who were working in the 1950s are not possible – those individuals would be a minimum of 85 to 100 years old today, unlikely still employed and unable to compare the state of access. Today's public access audits and empirical studies examining agency transparency provide good snapshots of access today, but were unheard of then. Scholars can examine the development of statutes and case law over time, as legal scholars conduct for specific access issues,[20] but

---

[17] SCHUDSON, *supra* note 2, at 16.

[18] Banisar, *supra* note 5, at 6.

[19] Lindita Camaj, *Gatekeeping the Gatekeepers: International Community and Freedom of Information in Kosovo,* 10 GLOBAL MEDIA J. 15 (2010).

[20] *See, e.g.*, Matthew D. Bunker & Charles N. Davis, *Privatized Government Functions and Freedom of Information: Public Accountability in an Age of Private Governance,* 75 JOURNALISM & MASS COMM. Q. 464 (1998) (discussing the practice by government to hide records through privatization of services); Meredith Fuchs, *Judging Secrets: The Role Courts Should Play in Preventing Unnecessary Secrecy,* 58 ADMIN. L. REV. 131 (2006) (discussing the history and law of the role of courts in freedom of information); Jonathan Peters & Edson C. Tandoc Jr., *"People Who Aren't Really Reporters at All, Who Have No Professional Qualifications": Defining a Journalist and Deciding Who May Claim the Privileges*, 34 N.Y.U. J. LEGIS. & PUB. POL'Y QUORUM 40 (2013) (a historical and legal analysis of how to define a "journalist" in regard to the law); Jeannine E. Relly & Carol B. Schwalbe, *How Business Lobby Networks Shaped the U.S. Freedom of Information Act: An Examination of 60 Years of Congressional Testimony,* GOV. INFO. Q. in press, *available at* http://www.sciencedirect.com/science/article/pii/S0740624X1630048X (last visited July 18, 2016) (an analysis of congressional testimony since the 1950s by business interests to influence FOIA).

these studies generally do not address actual access on the streets, nor do they examine freedom of information in a broad sense.

Given the relatively little research comparing pre-FOIA access to modern times, this study seeks to provide at least some glimpses through the examination of a written artifact from 1953 that offers a window into the state of access before Congress enacted FOIA: *The People's Right to Know* by Cross. The 405-page book, commissioned by the American Society of Newspaper Editors, was intended to lay out the state of access at all levels of government in the United States, including the statutes, case law and actual practice, as it existed in the early 1950s. Cross examined hundreds of court decisions regarding access,[21] studied the two dozen states that had some form of public record law at the time, and discussed the state of access to federal records. He also noted what journalists told him worked and what didn't work in practice.

This article begins by providing background for the post-World War II access movement and how Cross embarked on the study. The article then describes the state of public record access law in the 1950s at the state and federal level, as laid out by Cross, and compares his description to today's legal landscape. The discussion summarizes overall themes of how, based on Cross' report, transparency in the United States is stronger since the 1950s, how it is weaker, areas that have remained the same, and what journalists, access advocates and government officials can learn from the passage of time.

This study cannot determine causation – whether transparency laws have hindered or advanced one's ability to access government records. It also cannot determine whether access in practice is undeniably better or worse today than it was sixty years ago. This study can, however, provide some context for how the freedom of information landscape in the United States has evolved – legally and otherwise – since the beginning of the transparency movement and adoption of FOIA, by focusing on one significant historical artifact: the 1953 FOI "bible."[22]

THE PEOPLE'S RIGHT TO KNOW

Citizens' right to be informed about their government has been valued for millennia, at least as far back as the Athenians in 330 B.C.[23]

[21] CROSS, *supra* note 1, at 11.

[22] SCHUDSON, *supra* note 2, at 42 (referring to the work as "the much-cited bible of the freedom-of-information movement").

[23] *See* Shannon E. Martin & Gerry Lanosga, *The Historical Legal Underpinnings of Access to Public Documents,* 104 L. LIBR J. 614 (2010) (discussing historical background of how different governments approached transparency).

Chinese Emperor T'ai-tsung, who ruled in A.D. 627-49, espoused the virtues of government transparency and expected leaders to "admit their own imperfection as a proof for their love of the truth and in fear of ignorance and darkness."[24] These general principles began to take shape in the West in the 1700s, including passage December 2, 1766, of the world's first federal freedom of information and press rights legislation by what was then Sweden and Finland.[25]

American colonialists took up the right to know in their resistance against the British, but freedom of information was not explicitly stated in the U.S. Constitution, and even the practices of the founders sometimes contradicted the ideals of transparency.[26] Through the years, access to government information in the United States was dictated primarily by routine practices and common law, although glimpses into congressional intent for informing the public could be seen through such legislation as the Printing Act of 1895 and Federal Depository Library Act of 1962.[27]

The Supreme Court of the United States has been reluctant to acknowledge a constitutional right to know, and it wasn't until 1943 that it created a constitutional right to *receive* information in *Martin v. City of Struthers.*[28] By the mid-1900s, about half the states had adopted minimalistic statutes addressing document retention, and the federal government had enacted the Administrative Procedure Act in 1946,[29]

---

[24]Stephen Lamble, *Freedom of Information, a Finnish Clergyman's Gift to Democracy,* 97 FREEDOM OF INFO. REV. 3 (2002) (explaining how Anders Chydenius, the father of Sweden's FOIA law, referenced T'ai-tsung in his writings).

[25]The Freedom of the Press Act (1766) celebrates its 250th anniversary Dec. 2, 2016, as U.S. FOIA celebrated its fiftieth anniversary July 4, 2016. For translated text of Sweden's law, *see* http://www.chydenius.net/pdf/worlds_first_foia.pdf (last visited August 24, 2016).

[26]*See, e.g.,* Paul H. Gates Jr. & Bill F. Chamberlin, *Madison Misinterpreted: Historical Presentism Skews Scholarship,* 13 AM. JOURNALISM 38 (1996) (explaining how James Madison's quote about government without popular information as a "prologue to a farce or a tragedy" is often taken out of context); Martin E. Halstuk, *Policy of Secrecy – Pattern of Deception: What Federalist Leaders Thought About a Public Right to Know, 1794-98,* 7 COMM. L. & POL'Y 51 (2002) (examining how the founding fathers operated in secrecy soon after the creation of the nation); Martin & Lanosga, *supra* note 23, at 618 (discussing how Congress acted in secrecy in its early sessions, including the use of secret votes).

[27]*See* MARTIN, *supra* note 2, at 10 (explaining the early underpinnings of Congress to inform the public of its governance); Aimee C. Quinn, *Keeping the Citizenry Informed: Early Congressional Printing and 21st Century Information Policy,* 20 GOV. INFO. Q. 281 (2003) (providing a history of congressional intent on informing the public through dissemination of documents).

[28]319 U.S. 141 (1943).

[29]5 U.S.C. 1002, 60 Stat. 238 (1946).

ostensibly to help organize a growing bureaucracy, but often used to hide information.[30]

World War II noticeably affected the practice of accessing government information. Secrecy and censorship were seen as necessary in a mortal struggle for survival, where "loose lips sink ships." After the war ended in 1945, any hopes secrecy would be lifted were unfulfilled as anti-Communist fears continued to fuel national security measures. President Harry S. Truman exacerbated the situation by issuing an executive order in peace time to classify even more records as secret. Journalists began voicing their concerns in earnest.[31]

Sigma Delta Chi (now the Society of Professional Journalists) and the American Society of Newspaper Editors (now the American Society of News Editors) began receiving more and more requests for help from newspapers stymied by government roadblocks. ASNE FOI Committee Chairman James S. Pope, managing editor of the *Louisville Courier-Journal,* was baffled at what to tell fellow journalists. "We knew it was all wrong, but we didn't know how to start the battle for reformation,"[32] he said.

The ASNE FOI Committee initially started with a focus on international freedom of information but within a year of its founding in 1949 switched gears, noting in its report to members of the "growing tendency" of domestic bureaucrats high and low "to forget they are stewards of the people and to act instead as though taxpayers were their servants."[33] The committee aided, for example, an editor from Moose Lake, Minnesota, who requested vital statistics records from his county, was denied, objected in print, and then faced a libel suit filed by the county clerk. The editor won the suit with the help of ASNE.[34]

Frustrated at what he was seeing nationally, Pope felt stymied. "The mystery of the law had us fogbound," he said. "Who could pierce it?"[35] He reached out to Cross, an attorney for the *New York Herald Tribune* and professor at Columbia University's School of Journalism. The organization commissioned Cross to publish a report on the legal state of access to public records at all levels of government. Specifically, the organization wanted more information about the state of the law, what

---

[30]*See* CROSS, *supra* note 1, at 223-28; SCHUDSON, *supra* note 2, at 34, 57.

[31]*See* SCHUDSON, *supra* note 2, at 42.

[32]FOERSTEL, *supra* note 2, at 16.

[33]George Kennedy, Advocates of Openness: The Freedom of Information Movement 24 (August 1978) (unpublished Ph.D. dissertation, University of Missouri) (on file with University Microfilms International).

[34]*Id.* at 25.

[35]*Id.* at 30.

battles had been waged, who won, and how they won.[36] At their annual meeting in April 1951, ASNE leaders authorized Cross to conduct a "comprehensive report on customs, laws and court decisions affecting our free access to public information whether it is recorded on police blotters or in the files of the national government."[37]

The report would be the first of its kind. *Hartford Courant* Editor Herbert Brucker had published *Freedom of Information*[38] in 1949, a book espousing the need for a vibrant and free press, and Kent Cooper was credited by *The New York Times* as coining the phrase "right to know" in 1945, although Cooper primarily focused on propaganda and news suppression in other countries.[39] Nobody had yet outlined in detail the state of government access, legal or otherwise, in the United States. The undertaking was perhaps as daunting as the work of media law scholars today who painstakingly scour court decisions and statutes to describe the state of freedom of information law.[40]

Cross intended the report to serve newspaper editors, college students, media law attorneys and scholars, so he wrote for a broad audience.[41] His work resulted in a 405-page book that included an introduction to general access law provisions (that is, fees, enforcement), and chapters on the right of inspection, access to state and local records, police records, judicial records, judicial proceedings, administrative proceedings, and federal records. He included appendices to list court cases litigated by newspapers, the text of state open record laws, relevant court cases, attorneys general opinions, and federal regulations. He examined the statutes, constitutions, case law, attorneys general opinions, and regulations for the federal government, the forty-eight states, and the District of Columbia.

Because of the report, Cross became known as a national expert on freedom of information, providing testimony and written assistance at least twenty-six times to the Moss Committee charged with drafting a

---

[36] *See* CROSS, *supra* note 1, at xv.

[37] *Id.*

[38] HERBERT BRUCKER, FREEDOM OF INFORMATION 276 (1949) (This book did not focus on freedom of information in the sense that the term is used today, that is access to government records or proceedings. Brucker was more concerned about the press censorship he saw around the world and during World War II in the United States. He defines freedom of information as freedom for an independent and vibrant press, freedom from government control, or any attachment to any class, political party, economic group or other fraction of society.)

[39] *See* Kent Cooper's remarks from a speech, as executive director of *The Associated Press, cited in* Editorial, *The Right to Know,* N.Y. TIMES, Jan. 23, 1945, at 18. Cooper elaborated on his thoughts in his book eleven years later. KENT COOPER, THE RIGHT TO KNOW: AN EXPOSITION OF THE EVILS OF NEWS SUPPRESSION AND PROPAGANDA (1956).

[40] *See, e.g.,* RICHARD J. PELTZ-STEELE, THE LAW OF ACCESS TO GOVERNMENT (2012).

[41] CROSS, *supra* note 1, at xvi.

legislative amendment to the Administrative Practices Act. Cross, who died in 1959 at age 69, did not live to see that amendment, what is now called the Freedom of Information Act, signed into law, but Cross is credited with inspiring Moss to sponsor the legislation.[42]

Method

This study is based on an examination of each page of *The People's Right to Know* for all mentions of the state of access at the time – legally or in practice. It excluded two chapters regarding access to judicial proceedings and public meetings because of the focus on access to government records. In some cases the resulting data listed specific records that were considered open or closed at the time. In other cases, the data reflected the general landscape in records access, such as the definition of public records or legal limitations on the type of people permitted to request records.

Data were combined into similar groupings and then compared to the current state of access in the United States, based on published research and the "state compare" function of the Reporters Committee for Freedom of the Press fifty-state open government guide.[43] Conclusions are noted for areas that appear to have experienced increased access since the 1950s, areas that appear less transparent, and areas that appear the same.

FOI Landscape of 1953

As described by Cross, the legal landscape in 1953 for freedom of information was nascent, relying upon an amalgamation of young state laws, common law, case law, attorneys general opinions and agency regulations. About half the states at the time had general public record statutes providing a general right of inspection of records, according to Cross.[44] He wrote that there also were hundreds of other provisions

[42]*See* SCHUDSON, *supra* note 2, at 43 (Based on a letter between Moss and the American Society of Newspaper Editors, Moss traced the origins of the Freedom of Information Act to a conversation he had with Cross in 1954, when Cross suggested amending the Administrative Procedure Act of 1946).

[43]The *Open Government Guide* by the Reporters Committee for Freedom of the Press provides an online compare function for various elements of all states' public record laws, https://www.rcfp.org/open-government-guide (last visited July 13, 2016).

[44]CROSS, *supra* note 1, at 337-47. States were Alabama, Arizona, California, Florida, Georgia, Idaho, Illinois, Iowa, Kentucky, Louisiana, Massachusetts, Michigan, Minnesota, Montana, Nebraska, Nevada, New Hampshire, New Mexico, New York,

sprinkled throughout state laws regarding specific records, similar to today, but that he would focus only on statutes that provided an overall right of inspection.[45]

Cross wrote that in England, courts had declared that there was no general common law right for all persons to inspect public records. There was support for the right of inspection for use in litigation, and that migrated to the United States. Over time, courts started acknowledging purposes for public records other than litigation.[46] He wrote that there was no general common law right for just anyone to inspect records – typically only those who had a valid reason to see the information – although he noted that was changing in some states. Newspaper suits before 1900 generally were few and unsuccessful, but that was changing in the twentieth century.

Cross broke the states into three groups: (1) general inspection states (23) with laws creating a right to access records in general except for those records deemed secret;[47] (2) specific statute states (15) that specified what records would be public,[48] and (3) common law states (10) that had no laws and left it to common law practice.[49] Today all of the states would fit into the first category. Cross noted that the common law states were the least favorable toward journalists' access to records because they relied on the whims of agencies and trial judges. The District of Columbia had no general statute, but provided that certain records were public, such as property records and police logs.[50] Louisiana had the nation's most specific and comprehensive statute, Cross wrote,[51] although Florida had the strongest worded statute, even if shorter and more concise.

Cross suggested that new legislation should remove "moldy common law restrictions" concerning status, interest, motives and purposes of requesters, and limit judicial discretion to deny enforcement writs.[52]

North Carolina, Oklahoma, Oregon, South Dakota, Utah, Virginia, West Virginia and Wisconsin.

[45] *Id.* at 48-59.

[46] *Id.* at 26.

[47] *Id.* at 51. States were Alabama, Arizona, California, Florida, Georgia, Idaho, Iowa, Kentucky, Louisiana, Massachusetts, Michigan, Minnesota, Montana, Nebraska, Nevada, New Mexico, New York, North Carolina, Oklahoma, Oregon, South Dakota, Utah and Wisconsin.

[48] *Id.* at 53. States were Colorado, Connecticut, Illinois, Indiana, Kansas, Mississippi, Missouri, North Dakota, Ohio, Pennsylvania, Tennessee, Texas, Virginia, Washington and Wyoming.

[49] *Id.* at 54. States were Arkansas, Delaware, Maryland, Maine, New Hampshire, New Jersey, Rhode Island, South Carolina, Vermont and West Virginia.

[50] *Id.* at 55.

[51] *Id.* at 8.

[52] *Id.* at 58.

The right of inspection, in general, at that time had been applied by statute to specific records, such as those related to elections, fees, salaries, revenues, title to property, judicial proceedings, and other areas where any member of a community would have a legitimate interest in them.[53]

Also, at the time, newspapers were still fighting for fundamental press freedoms, such as the battles against prior restraint and criminal libel. For example, Cross notes, some states still employed "You Can't Print That" statutes, which allowed access to records but prohibited the publication of certain information. Wisconsin had a statute, for example, prohibiting publication of the names of female rape victims that were available in public records.[54] Also, most state courts did not consider all public records as privileged in the case of libel lawsuits, such as judicial records that had been filed but not yet the subject of judicial action or disposition. Some states were beginning to move away from that, Cross noted, considering all public records as privileged documents in libel cases.[55]

In general, Cross found what he perceived as a shift toward secrecy at all levels of government. For example, income tax records had been considered open to public inspection in some cases, but were being closed. He also noted an increased shift toward secrecy in judicial records and documents regarding family relationships – divorce, juvenile court, domestic relations, family, youthful offender, wayward minor, marriage and support of dependents.

However, he found a general improvement in access developing through statutes, such as broadening the definition of "public records," which previously had been restricted to those specifically made public by law, or those records having specific relevance to an individual requester. Cross wrote that there were two kinds of court decisions: (1) rulings interpreting statutes, which often did not go well for requesters because the statutes were not well-developed – "The applicant might have been better off at common law. A statute is not always a help;"[56] and (2) Rulings applying common law where statutes did not exist.

Without many statutes to guide agencies, journalists or the courts, Cross noted that a growing type of access law was in "official regulations," where agencies created their own processes and policies, particularly at the federal level. Many state statutes granted officials

[53]*Id.* at 65.
[54]*Id.* at 17.
[55]*Id.* at 17-18.
[56]*Id.* at 22.

authority to issue regulations on access to records.[57] This, he says, is where journalists ran into problems.

Definition of "Public Record"

Cross listed fifteen states that had outlined in statute the definition of a "public record," although the laws were generally vague and tended to focus on the creation and retention of "writings."[58] Louisiana's statute was most detailed, and included a list of records to be made available and kept secret.[59] Cross described Louisiana's lengthy law as "useful, convenient, and liberal," and "well-liked by newsmen."[60] In states that did not provide a statutory definition, courts created their own interpretation through case law, some better than others.[61] For example, Indiana's Supreme Court defined a "public record" as a document *required by law* "to be kept,"[62] which created problems for requesters. Legally, a record would not be public unless specifically mentioned by statute, court rule, or attorney general opinion to be maintained by the government. This excluded the bulk of documents.[63] Cross noted a better approach, which is more representative of definitions today: Wisconsin's courts created the broadest definition of a public record as anything created and held by government.[64]

Cross also noted that there were thousands of state statutes regarding access to specific records sprinkled throughout state laws, such as access to juvenile court records or auto registration records. He chose to focus on the records most relevant to newspapers.[65] Also, he noted that someone needed to look at all the statutes to find exemptions, given the growing legal terminology that records would be public "except as otherwise provided by statute."[66] Ultimately, Cross wrote that the definition of public record was a problem in most states – dependent on accident of statute or the intent with which the record was made. "The right should

[57] *Id.* at 23.

[58] *Id.* at 38-47. States with statutes defining public records were California, Delaware, Idaho, Illinois, Kansas, Louisiana, Maryland, Massachusetts, Montana, New Jersey, North Carolina, Oregon, Tennessee, Texas and Utah.

[59] *Id.* at 328-36.

[60] *Id.* at 39.

[61] *Id.* at 21.

[62] *Id.* at 43.

[63] *Id.* at 33.

[64] *Id.* at 44.

[65] *Id.* at 21.

[66] *Id.* at 34.

depend on the status of the document as a record of exercise of official functions,"[67] he wrote.

Today the definitions of "public records" at the federal and state levels have more clarity, in line with what Cross had suggested, typically including any recorded materials — including video, audio or electronic — created or held by a government agency.[68] In this respect, citizen access has improved since 1953. Still, issues continue to arise, including the myriad of exemptions for specific types of records,[69] and emerging technological issues, such as whether records sent from officials' private cell phones or email accounts are subject to public record laws.[70]

Who Can Inspect Records

Cross noted that in 1953 most jurisdictions factored into their record release the type of person asking to see a record and the purpose of the request. This was based on the common law notion, Cross wrote, that records were provided only for purposes that were "lawful, proper or legitimate."[71] Some people not allowed to see public records included those "with a destructive or other unlawful purpose."[72] In addition, some state statutes limited requesters to certain legal standing. For

[67] *Id.* at 47.

[68] For example, the definition of a record in U.S. FOIA is, "Any information that would be an agency record subject to the requirements of this section when maintained by an agency in any format, including an electronic format; and (B) any information described under subparagraph (A) that is maintained for an agency by an entity under Government contract, for the purposes of records management." 5 U.S.C. § 552(f)(2) (2016).

[69] Exemption b(3) in the Freedom of Information Act allows for records to be kept secret under individual statutes passed by Congress; therefore, hundreds of exemptions have been added throughout federal statutes. Access advocates identify this exemption as one of the most difficult to control because secrecy provisions find themselves in any bill. *See, e.g.,* Jennifer LaFleur, Al Shaw & Jeff Larson, *FOIA b(3) Exemptions,* PRO PUBLICA, http://projects.propublica.org/foia-exemptions/ (last visited July 13, 2016) (showing prevalence of different exemptions by agency, including making secret information about watermelon handlers, avocado importers and caves).

[70] *See, e.g.,* Joey Senat, *Whose Business Is It: Is Public Business Conducted on Officials' Personal Electronic Devices Subject to State Open Records Laws?*, 19 COMM. L. & POL'Y 293 (2014) (examining how the states, through statute and case law, view access to public officials work-related communications *via* personal phone or email); Kyu Ho Youm, *Access to Email and the Right of Privacy in the Workplace, in* DAXTON STEWART ED., SOCIAL MEDIA AND THE LAW: A GUIDEBOOK FOR COMMUNICATION STUDENTS AND PROFESSIONALS 97 (2012) (examining case law concerning access to government officials' email communications).

[71] CROSS, *supra* note 1, at 36.

[72] *Id.* at 14.

example, New York limited access to "taxpayers," Florida to "citizens," and Louisiana to "elector or taxpayer."[73]

New statutes, however, were beginning to broaden who had a right to inspect records, Cross wrote.[74] This broadening was pushed by commercial interests who wanted access to records, particularly title records, for doing business. Colorado and Kansas, for example, provided special access to title companies for records and nobody else.[75] He noted that Pennsylvania courts ruled that no particular reason was needed to see a record, and the right may be exercised even out of "idle curiosity."[76] Tennessee courts ruled that political hostility to the government is no excuse for refusing inspection.[77]

Journalists were generally seen as favored requesters in the 1950s and often received better service than other citizens. Cross made a case that journalists should be treated differently than others, particularly in a chapter he dedicated to "Newspapers as Litigants."[78] He argued that newspapers had been generally successful in winning lawsuits because the news function has a "sufficient special interest."[79] Also, he argued that newspapers do not act out of idle curiosity, do not sell records to disadvantage agencies, do not clutter up records offices, rarely demand sweeping inspection of all records, and do not harass. "In short," he wrote, "in general the newspaper purpose is lawful."[80] Further, Cross noted lower court rulings that suggested the press had a First Amendment right to access public records and attend government proceedings, and he expressed hope the Supreme Court would enshrine such a constitutional right to accessing public records.[81] That has yet to come to pass.

Today, the state of access is better in this area, because few states distinguish between requesters or purpose, or impose limitations on citizenry, let alone voting status or tax-paying status.[82] Some states impose

[73]*Id.* at 15.
[74]*Id.* at 16.
[75]*Id.* at 53.
[76]*Id.* at 36.
[77]*Id.*
[78]*Id.* at 122-32.
[79]*Id.* at 123.
[80]*Id.* at 123.
[81]*Id.* at 10.
[82]Arizona Public Records Law gives "any person" the right inspect public records. ARIZ. REV. STAT. ANN. § 39-121 (2016). Similar wording is present in public record statutes of California, Colorado, Connecticut, District of Columbia, Florida, Hawaii, Idaho, Illinois, Indiana, Iowa, Kansas, Kentucky, Massachusetts, Minnesota, Mississippi, Montana, Nebraska, Nevada, New Hampshire, New Mexico, North Carolina, North Dakota, Ohio, Oklahoma, Oregon, Rhode Island, South Carolina, South Dakota, Texas, Utah, West Virginia and Wyoming.

restrictions on prison inmates,[83] and those who are not citizens of the state or the United States.[84] Also, as a sign that *all* citizens should be treated equally, today for the most part journalists have no special legal treatment in accessing records, except for expedited processing and lower fees in federal FOIA.[85]

Penalties for Agency Noncompliance

Cross lamented that the only recourse journalists and citizens had when denied records was granted through common law: writ of mandamus. He provided several examples of how this put the citizen at a disadvantage, forcing a person to hire an attorney and take the time to sue civilly, and, therefore, that the right of access was "absolute in theory" but "qualified in practice."[86]

Five state statutes included criminal penalties against public officials who did not follow the law. North Carolina and West Virginia declared a violation a misdemeanor.[87] Alabama provided for a fine of not less than $50 for any public officer not allowing any person to examine a record free of charge.[88] Florida made officials subject to removal or impeachment and guilty of a misdemeanor punishable by fine or imprisonment.[89] Louisiana made it a misdemeanor punishable by fine or imprisonment, or for willful destruction or concealment a crime punishable "by imprisonment at hard labor in the penitentiary."[90] Cross noted no punishment at the federal level, or for judicial records.

[83]Washington State's statute imposes restrictions on inmates, including the courts' ability to impose injunctions preventing inmates from submitting public record requests. REV. CODE WASH. § 42.56.565 (2016) was upheld in *Franklin County Sheriff's Office v. Parmelee*, 285 P. 3d 67 (Wash. 2012). Arkansas, as well, prohibits incarcerated felons from obtaining records from the Department of Corrections. *See* ARK. CODE ANN. § 25-19-105(a)(1) (2016).

[84]*See, e.g.,* McBurney v. Young, 122 S.Ct. 1709 (2013) (unanimously upholding the Virginia public record law that limited requests to citizens of the state, saying noncitizens don't foot the bill for records and do not have an interest in scrutinizing governments they do not live under. Justice Samuel Alito wrote, "This Court has repeatedly made clear that there is no constitutional right to obtain all the information provided by FOIA laws." *Id.* at 1718).

[85]*See* 5 U.S.C. § 552 (2016). *See* specifically 4(A) ii. II dictating reasonable fees for the news media, scientific research, and other noncommercial uses. *See also* 6(E) regarding expedited processing for those who can demonstrate a "compelling need."

[86]CROSS, *supra* note 1, at 31.

[87]*Id.* at 344.

[88]*Id.* at 337.

[89]*Id.* at 338.

[90]*Id.* at 333.

In an examination of access law enforcement provisions in 2010, Daxton "Chip" Stewart found that today nearly every jurisdiction has some form of enforcement mechanism. All but sixteen states provide for some kind of civil or criminal penalty, including jail time in some cases. Many allow for award of attorney fees for successful plaintiffs, and sometimes punitive damages.[91] Stewart wrote, echoing Cross, "However, the practical availability of these remedies makes them problematic."[92] Citizens face the same issues today as they did in 1953: Hiring a lawyer to take on city hall can be expensive, time-consuming and intimidating. Even news organizations are less likely to sue for public records today because of time and resource constraints.[93] The system remains stacked against the requester, as it was in 1953.

Fees and the Right to Copy

In general, statutes and common law were broad enough to allow anyone to copy, extract or photograph records that they inspected, Cross noted. However, he did not specify whether the laws addressed copy fees.[94] In parts of the book, he wrote that some agencies earned revenue from record copies, but did not note that fees were a barrier for the press or citizens, perhaps because machine copies were relatively new in 1953 (the first Xerox machine was introduced in 1949). Today

[91]Washington State, for example, allows judges to award up to $100 per day for each day the requester was denied the record. REV. CODE WASH. § 42.56.505(4) (2016). In 2003, the former mayor of Mesa, Washington, sued over denial of records and won a judgment of $353,000 in penalties, reduced in 2016 to $175,000, the judge citing a concern that the payout would bankrupt the farm town of 500 people. *See* Wendy Culverwell, *Judge Slashes Penalty in Mesa Public Records Case,* TRI-CITY HERALD, July 1, 2016, *available at* http://www.tri-cityherald.com/news/local/article86976727.html (last visited July 18, 2016).

[92]Daxton "Chip" Stewart, *Let the Sunshine In, or Else: An Examination of the "Teeth" of State and Federal Open Meetings and Open Records Laws,* 15 COMM. L. & POL'Y 298 (2010).

[93]In a Knight Foundation survey of sixty-six news editors in 2016, two-thirds said news organizations were less likely to sue for First Amendment issues than they were ten years ago. *See* In Defense of the First Amendment: U.S. News Leaders Feel Less Able to Confront Issues in Court in the Digital Age, *available at* http://www.knightfoundation.org/press-room/press-release/news-organizations-ability-champion-first-amendmen/ (last visited July 18, 2016). Also, similar findings were reported in a 2009 Open Government Survey by the Media Law Research Center and National Freedom of Information Coalition, *available at* http://www.nfoic.org/uploads/foi_pdfs/MLRC-NFOIC-Open-Govt-Survey.pdf (last visited July 13, 2016).

[94]CROSS, *supra* note 1, at 34-35.

excessive fees, particularly for search and redaction time, can be problematic for requesters, more so than in 1953.[95]

Access to Specific Record Categories

Cross identified records and that were deemed public or secret. In addition to addressing specific records, he provided a list of eighty-two types of records and their status as opened or closed.[96] For the most part they mirrored the laws and practices of today, but in some cases certain types of records were open that aren't open today, and in other cases records were more restrictive than today.

Similarities to Today

Records deemed secret then, as today, included those involving national security, diplomatic correspondence, and communications by government informants.[97] Others included records of heads of states (that is, president or governors),[98] and catch-all exemptions where release would be detrimental to the public interest.[99] Some records were considered inherently secret because they contained information deemed private, including medical and mental records in state institutions, tax records, "correspondence between officials in certain circumstances," and certain vital statistics.[100] Records that were routinely available then, as today, included county board of supervisor records,

[95]*See* Tae Ho Lee, *Public Records Fees Hidden in the Law: A Study of Conflicting Judicial Approaches to the Determination of the Scope of Imposable Public Records Fees,* 21 COMM. L. & POL'Y 251 (2016) (pointing out that laws are inconsistent and agencies often vague in what they charge to requesters); Emily Grannis, *Paying for Public Access: FOI Fees Add Up For Journalists Trying to Explain Government Activities,* NEWS MEDIA & L., Spring 2014, at 3, *available at* http://www.rcfp.org/browse-media-law-resources/news-media-law/news-media-and-law-spring-2014/paying-public-access (last visited July 13, 2016) (noting problems of growing fees as barriers to obtaining records); Anna Clark, *How 'The Public is Priced Out of Public Records' By Michigan Universities,* COLUM. JOURNALISM R., Apr. 5, 2016, *available at* http://www.cjr.org/united_states_project/how_the_public_is_priced_out_of_public_records_by_michigan_universities.php (last visited July 13, 2016) (discussing universities that wanted to charge more than $20,000 to students requesting public records for an FOI audit); Nick Grube, *Many States Charge Insane Fees For Access To Public Records,* HUFFINGTON POST, Oct. 17, 2013, http://www.huffingtonpost.com/2013/10/17/fees-for-public-records_n_4119049.html (last visited July 13, 2016) (points out examples of exorbitant fees charged to journalists).

[96]CROSS, *supra* note 1, Appendix 4, at 348-54.

[97]*Id.* at 6.

[98]*Id.* at 80.

[99]*Id.* at 81.

[100]*Id.* at 18.

salary books, jail records, budgets, alcohol sale licenses and state fire marshal findings.[101]

More Restrictive in 1953

Records deemed closed in 1953 that would likely be available today in most jurisdictions included automobile accident reports, which were available only to those involved in the accident. Hearings and records involving juvenile courts were generally considered secret, or open only to those who involved.[102] In many states today that information is public. Records under common law that generally were not regarded as important to the public or journalists, and therefore kept secret, included real estate deeds, mortgages, probated wills, and money judgments rendered in courts,[103] which are routinely made public today. Some states in 1953 withheld records that would compete with the revenue of an agency. [104]

Simple communications in writing passing between officials could be kept secret, and there was no general right of inspection of records of executive departments that were kept merely as evidence of transactions in departments.[105] This speaks to what many jurisdictions consider today as the "deliberative" exemption (that is, Exemption 5 in FOIA), to allow for free and open exchanges in private before final actions are considered. However, in many jurisdictions today requesters have had success, for example, in acquiring routine email communications among city council members.

Vital statistics regarding marriage, birth, death and divorce, were being increasingly restricted to those who had a particular status or need, Cross wrote. [106] Some sixteen states had adopted the Uniform Vital Statistics Act policies to limit disclosure of these records to those

---

[101]*Id.* at 66. (Cross lists dozens of records deemed public by various agencies' statutes or case law, including auditor bills (Vermont, 1906), tax collection records (Alabama, 1882), expenditures of public funds for entertainment of conference of governors (Michigan, 1928), dental examiners board examination papers (Florida, 1940), city tax records (Tennessee, 1903), public works records (New York, 1933), financial records of a county (Texas, 1915), meeting minutes, ordinances (Missouri, 1936, Connecticut, 1950), death records except strong trend toward increased secrecy (New York, 1892), contracts (Alabama, 1895), action by smoke control board, with complainant names redacted (New York, 1951), health department final reports, but not investigative reports (California, 1951), marriage licenses with some exceptions toward trend in secrecy (Michigan, 1907), jail records (Alabama, 1941), and property assessment records (Illinois, 1943)).

[102]*Id.* at 7.

[103]*Id.* at 15.

[104]*Id.*

[105]*Id.* at 78.

[106]*Id.* at 7.

with a "direct interest in the matter."[107] He saw this as a growing trend toward closure, and that the press largely was apathetic in pushing back. These restrictions continue today in some states, but not all. Divorce records are generally available to the public in most jurisdictions today through the courts.

Health department records were all secret, except for statistics, which made it difficult to verify the statistics, Cross noted.[108] While medical and private information pertaining to individuals might be kept secret today, other health department information often is released, such as restaurant inspection reports.

Some records were kept secret if they were not officially required by statute to be kept, even if the agency maintained the records. That was the case in Washington State, Kentucky and New Jersey. For example, a report on the conditions of a police department was held non-public because no statute required it to be filed or recorded.[109] Other records deemed secret by court or statute, often because there was no law saying they had to be kept, included applications for grazing (Montana, 1921), probate indices (Ohio, 1946), redemption of lands from tax sales (Washington, 1905), city engineer records (Kentucky, 1913), and a report by the attorney general to governor regarding an investigation of the state land commissioner (Arizona, 1951).[110]

Cross devoted an entire chapter to the problems in acquiring police records – the only chapter focused on a specific type of record.[111] He noted that the key to getting this sort of information rested with good sourcing between journalists and police officials: "Sugar, plus judicious admixtures of strength and determination, catches more 'police news' than vinegar."[112] Cross wrote, however, that the law should be better. He described it as divergent, restrictive, obscure and nonexistent. Few court decisions and an excess of dicta in judicial opinions and loose definitions were causing mass confusion. New York City, for example, considered all police records secret, including blotter information – leaving reporters to rely on relationships with officers to get information. Meanwhile, in other parts of the state journalists could get full access to police records. Louisiana state law explicitly directed police to explain the cause of jailing and make that open to anyone. Other jurisdictions fell somewhere between New York City and Louisiana.[113] Much case

[107] *Id.* at 93.
[108] *Id.* at 87.
[109] *Id.* at 77.
[110] *Id.* at 81-83.
[111] *Id.* at 95-121 (Chapter 8: Police Records).
[112] *Id.* at 96.
[113] *Id.* at 98.

law indicated that records could be kept secret until the matter was settled in open court, or until the police were done with their investigation and it entered the courts, typical of today's "investigatory" exemptions in most state laws.

Cross advocated that specific well-defined instructions be adopted by statute to clear up the confusion. Barring better statutes, Cross urged news companies to sue for access, highlighting the fact the long custom of providing the information informally. He also suggested more specificity in police record definitions so routine crime descriptions would not be deemed secret as investigatory evidence or informant records.[114]

More Open in 1953

Records considered open in 1953 but generally secret in today's world included motor vehicle registration and, in some states, drivers' licenses.[115] Cross noted a general trend toward secrecy with these records, mainly because officials saw the requests as a nuisance.[116] Eventually these records would become private because of the Driver's Privacy Protection Act of 1994[117] and its backing by the Supreme Court in *Reno v. Condon*.[118] Other open records included school census records, which are often kept secret today because of the Family Educational Right to Privacy Act.[119]

Public assistance program records[120] were sometimes open for inspection, including the lists of vagrants lodged at city expense. Given the relative newness of federal and state social programs, agencies were working through the issues. The federal Bureau of Unemployment Security had started divvying out matching funds to states with the requirement that they keep the information secret. This spread to other programs, such as welfare relief records, Cross wrote. When journalists exposed fraud in the programs, states began repealing the secrecy laws to foster transparency and accountability. Congress passed the Jenner amendment, for example, to repeal mandatory secrecy provisions of the Social Security Act, leading to a better-run system in eliminating

[114]*Id.* at 121.
[115]*Id.* at 67-68.
[116]*Id.* at 88.
[117]18 U.S. Code § 2721 (2016).
[118]528 U.S. 141 (2000). *See also* Joey Senat, Reno v. Condon *Opens Door to More Access Limits,* 24 NEWSPAPER RES. J. 63 (2003).
[119]20 U.S. Code § 1232g; 34 CFR Part 99 (2016).
[120]CROSS, *supra* note 1, at 18.

unqualified recipients. Cross anticipated, though, secrecy would return, which it did.[121]

Judicial Records

Cross dedicated a chapter to judicial records and a chapter to judicial proceedings. This might seem odd today because judicial records are generally not subject to public record statutes; rather, most states allow courts to develop their own rules. However, at the time, Cross wrote, many states that had statutes regulating access to records had broad enough language to include court records.[122] This was particularly true where county clerks were the legal custodians of judicial records.

Cross noted that the general philosophy at the time was that nearly all judicial records were open to anyone through common law, though some court definitions clarified that "this does not mean that inspection is for every one or mere pastime, whim or fancy."[123] Cross expressed puzzlement by the courts' fear of people reading through judicial records for salacious details about their co-workers, neighbors and family members. This mirrors a similar debate today of whether to post electronic court records online, lest "jammie surfers" scour the Internet from the comfort of their basements for dirt on their friends and family.[124]

Typical judicial records deemed public in 1953 included affidavits, lawsuits, court opinions, fee books, indictments, jury rolls, warrants, and records of proceedings, including witness testimony.[125] Records not deemed public involved adoptions, attachments in civil actions involving private information, attorney disbarment or suspension, coroners' records (although inquests were open), divorce litigation (although it appeared to be opening up a little because of changes in societal norms),[126] domestic relations records, and juvenile court records. Courts were provided the ability to seal records as they deemed fit.

[121]*Id.* at 89-90. The Social Security Act, 42 U.S.C. § 1397 (2016), provides confidentiality for those on public assistance.

[122]*Id.* at 139 (states noted by Cross were Arizona, California, Idaho, Louisiana, Montana, Oregon and Utah, Tennessee, Illinois and Virginia).

[123]*Id.* at 136.

[124]*See* Richard J. Peltz-Steele, *Electronic Court Record Access: Present Landscape, Neutral Principles, and the Looming Interloper of Contextual Privacy, in* CHARLES N. DAVIS & DAVID CUILLIER, TRANSPARENCY 2.0: DIGITAL DATA AND PRIVACY IN A WIRED WORLD 70 (2014) (examining the courts' reasoning for "practical obscurity," where requesters are forced to physically go to courthouses to see court records rather than online to avoid casual snooping by jammie surfers).

[125]CROSS, *supra* note 1, at 142.

[126]*Id.* at 147-48.

Cross concluded that the right to access judicial records, with some exceptions, was clear, strong and dependable.

Not a lot has changed since 1953 regarding judicial records, other than the establishment of court rules to regulate judicial record access, and some opening of records previously deemed sensitive. For example, divorce records today are predominantly open to public inspection unless sealed for special reasons. Also, in many states today, juvenile criminal records and proceedings are public.

Federal Records

The People's Right to Know has 247 pages of text followed by 158 pages of notes and appendices. Only fifty-three of those 405 total pages are dedicated to accessing federal records. The reason is made clear in the beginning of Chapter 8: "The dismaying, bewildering fact is that in the absence of a general or specific act of Congress creating a clear right to inspect – and such acts are not numerous – there is no enforceable legal right in public or press to inspect any federal non-judicial record."[127] Basically, there wasn't much for Cross to write about because the access landscape at the federal level was bleak.

Records of the executive department were considered "quasi-confidential" and "privileged communications."[128] Administrative agencies provided documents to the public only when it served their purposes. Departmental rules and regulations provided for some access to some records and hearings, but it was at the discretion of the agency head if he or she determined the information of "public interest" and "compatible with the welfare of society."[129]

Cross outlined the reasons for the lack of legal teeth for requesters to inspect federal records about the executive branch:

1. Separation of powers prevented the courts from compelling the president or executive department heads to provide information. Examples of records kept secret included investigative reports of executive departments, and the president had refused to disclose to Congress numerous other records.[130] The courts also held that the question of whether records would be against the public interest should be up to the executive branch to decide, not for

[127] *Id.* at 197.
[128] *Id.* at 198.
[129] *Id.* at 199.
[130] *Id.* at 205.

the courts. This power had not been fully tested, but Cross wrote, "It should be."[131]

2. A line of attorneys general opinions concluded that executive department records were privileged communications. Some records kept secret because of that included correspondence between officials concerning violations of internal revenue law.
3. The Administrative Procedure Act of 1946 specifically allowed departments to come up with their own rules, and provided a sweeping exception to disclosure for "any matter relating solely to the internal management of an agency."[132] This is similar to Exemption 5 in FOIA and deliberative exemptions in state laws today, which remain problematic for requesters.
4. Other actions by Congress kept federal records secret, similar to Exemption b(3) in FOIA, adoption of the Driver's Privacy Protection Act, the Family Educational Right and Privacy Act, the Health Insurance Portability and Accountability Act, and the thousands of exemptions sprinkled throughout state laws.
5. A dearth of court decisions at the federal level.[133] Cross mentioned, as well, the use of the "state secrets" privilege by the president to keep records secret, even from the courts.

Cross noted the increasing congressional impatience with the growing secrecy in the executive branch. "Change must come, and the time is ripe to accept the challenge," he wrote. "The primary forum is Congress. Relief in the courts is by no means hopeless."[134] Cross noted that he found not a single lawsuit where a newspaper sued for access to federal records. Cross did not address secrecy in military censorship or in the field of atomic energy, a sensitive area of the time given the recent detonation of the atomic bomb and growing Cold War fears.

Cross outlined the broad scope of records specifically kept secret under the Administrative Procedure Act of 1946, listing seventy-nine examples, including diplomatic codes, trade secrets, cotton and tobacco data, census records, oil and natural gas records, tax returns, and investigations of investment companies. In general, many of the records, particularly those involving privacy and national security, would be considered exempt through common law, Cross wrote. On the other hand, the Administrative Procedure Act did provide for certain records to be made public, including the names and contributions of

[131] *Id.* at 200.
[132] *Id.* at 211.
[133] *Id.* at 201.
[134] *Id.* at 202.

lobbyists, farm acreage allotments, Customs Court decisions, collective bargaining agreements and coal mine safety conditions.

The statutes, however, had relatively small impact on access, Cross argued, compared to departmental and agency regulations – the discretion of departments to essentially set their own disclosure rules. The Department of Justice regulations stated:

> All official files, documents, records and information in the offices of the Department of Justice, including the several offices of the United States Attorneys, Federal Bureau of Investigation, United States Marshals and Federal penal and correctional institutions, or in the custody or control of any officer or employee of the Department of Justice, are to be regarded as confidential.[135]

The regulations also instructed government employees to decline any subpoena for records.

Regarding the federal government, Cross provided these recommendations:

1. The access community should argue a First Amendment justification to access official information, and the Supreme Court should determine that access to government information is a First Amendment right.[136] The Supreme Court to this day has yet to acknowledge a constitutional right to access government documents.
2. Courts, not the executive branch, should have the power to determine whether information should be kept secret. Significant case law has since been established since 1953, although evidence suggests the courts still defer to the executive branch and respect separation of powers, particularly in cases involving national security.[137]
3. Congress should pass a new law, or at least amend the Administrative Procedure Act. This happened thirteen years after his book's publication, in 1966, with the APA amendment, referred to today as the Freedom of Information Act.

---

[135] *Id.* at 240.

[136] *Id.* at 219.

[137] *See, e.g.,* Derigan Silver, *Power, National Security and Transparency: Judicial Decision Making and Social Architecture in the Federal Courts,* 15 COMM. L. & POL'Y 129 (2010) (analyzing Supreme Court cases involving free press, free expression, and transparency balanced with national security to find malleability in how justices reach their conclusions).

While not all of Cross' suggestions have come to fruition, particularly the affirmation of a First Amendment right to access public records, great strides have been made since 1953 in the ability for citizens to access information from federal executive agencies.

Discussion

Freedom of information law was nascent in the 1950s as fledgling statutes, case law, attorney general opinions, agency regulations, and common practices swirled about in a bubbling pool, eventually evolving into what we have today. Cross provided the most comprehensive description at the time of the legal landscape for local, state and federal jurisdictions. His observations provide a basis for some comparison to the state of access today.

First, in many ways the state of access in 1953 was similar to what citizens and journalists experience today. Common law principles for what should be available and what should be secret in 1953 eventually became enshrined in court cases, FOIA in 1966, and a flurry of state public record laws in the early 1970s, following public discontent from Watergate, Vietnam and the civil rights movement.

For the most part, access is better today because of more defined laws and rules, particularly in the area of police reports, federal records, judicial records, and in the process of accessing public records – the definition of public records, the open nature of who can request records, and the breadth of government information available to the public. Some records, such as automobile accident reports, divorce records and public communications by officials, are easier to access today in many jurisdictions.

A key improvement in access over the past sixty years has been the shift toward a presumption of openness. Rather than dictating what records can be made public, as stipulated by common law and many statutes in 1953, current law assumes all government records are available to public inspection unless there are statutes that specify reasons for secrecy. That presumption was most recently codified at the federal level through the FOIA Improvement Act of 2016.[138]

Further, state public record laws in 1953 were either nonexistent or vague, with more than half the states relying on common law, their own rules and regulations, or releasing records only if there was a law specifically saying the record should be public. Today, local and state agencies

[138]FOIA Improvement Act, S. 337, 114th Cong. (2016).

must follow state public record laws, and cannot create regulations that counter those laws.

Interestingly, however, the detail and length of a state public record law might not be as important as the strength of its language. In 1953, Cross applauded Louisiana's public record law for its detail, yet today similar detailed laws are not always the strongest – often including elaborate and numerous exemptions for what should be kept secret. Florida, on the other hand, started with a succinct law that essentially dictated that all government records are presumed public, with some rare exceptions. This strong and concise wording could have led to what many consider the strongest public record law in the nation today.[139]

Access to federal records, while often frustrating, is clearly better in the twenty-first century than it was in 1953, when very little federal information was available to the public unless an agency wished to divulge it proactively for its own purposes. Today, the federal government receives nearly three-quarters of a million FOIA requests a year,[140] and information released because of FOIA has led to important public revelations.[141]

Despite improvements in freedom of information law, in some respects access has worsened over time, or remains at a state that frustrates journalists today as it did then. Increasing fees for record searches, retrieval, redaction, and copies – not mentioned at all by Cross in his book – hobble requesters today.[142] A variety of records that were available in 1953, such as motor vehicle registration, public welfare rolls and vital records are secret today, primarily because of increased concern for personal privacy.

Lack of enforcement of public record laws remains as salient today as it was in 1953. A nation or state can have the best access provisions on the books, but they are useless if ignored. Government and the access

[139]Journalists often point to Florida as the gold standard in public record laws. *See, e.g.,* Susannah Nesmith, *Florida's Public Records Law is Strong: Here are 5 Ways Lawmakers Want to Weaken It*, COLUM. JOURNALISM REV., Mar. 19, 2015, *available at* http://www.cjr.org/united_states_project/florida_public_records_bills.php (last visited July 18, 2016). However, some national rankings of state transparency place Florida in the bottom half of the country. *See, e.g.,* The Center for Public Integrity 2015 rankings for public access to information, *available at* https://www.publicintegrity.org/2015/11/03/18822/how-does-your-state-rank-integrity (last visited July 13, 2016).

[140]Specifically, 713,168 FOIA requests were submitted to the federal government in 2015, according to the U.S. Department of Justice, https://www.foia.gov/index.html (last visited July 13, 2016).

[141]Seven-hundred news stories benefited from FOIA requests, according to the Sunshine in Government Initiative's FOIA Files project, *available at* http://sunshineingovernment.org/wordpress/the-foia-files/ (last visited July 13, 2016).

[142]*See supra* note 95.

community should continue to work through new and better ways of making the system work.

Also, Cross' dream of seeing the courts acknowledge a constitutional right to access records has not come to fruition. Meanwhile, some states and nations have incorporated a right to access government information in their constitutions. The U.S. Supreme Court has dipped its toes in those waters, such as acknowledging a constitutional right for the press to attend some court proceedings,[143] but more remains to be done to make the constitutional right to know a reality.

Finally, fears expressed by Cross in 1953 of encroaching secrecy serve as relevant warnings for today. He surmised that government was becoming more secretive because of habits developed in government from World War II, a growing right of privacy as expounded by Samuel Warren and Louis Brandeis,[144] successful advocacy in legislatures by social workers to close vital records, and, "A tendency on the part of the press, under pressure of other problems, to let adverse trends go unchallenged."[145]

His observations resonate today. The United States experienced increased secrecy following the Iraq War, and national security measures furthered by former President George W. Bush.[146] Scholars and journalists have noted increased secrecy in the past thirty years because of public fears about privacy invasion,[147] and increased pressures by special interest groups to close records.[148]

---

[143]Press-Enterprise v. Superior Court, 478 U.S. 1 (1986) (providing a First Amendment right for press to attend preliminary hearings in criminal cases); Press-Enterprise v. Superior Court, 464 U.S. 501 (1984) (providing a First Amendment right for press to attend jury selection); Richmond Newspapers v. Virginia, 448 U.S. 555 (1980) (acknowledging a First Amendment right for the press to attend criminal trials).

[144]Samuel Warren & Louis Brandeis, *The Right to Privacy,* 4 HARV. L. R. 193 (1890).

[145]CROSS, *supra* note 1, at 12-13.

[146]*See* Jane E. Kirtley, *Transparency and Accountability in a Time of Terror: The Bush Administration's Assault of Freedom of Information,* 11 COMM. L. & POL'Y 479 (2006) (outlining actions taken by the administration of George W. Bush to increase secrecy following the terrorist attacks of Sept. 11, 2001). *See also* Seth F. Kreimer, *Rays of Sunlight in a Shadow "War": FOIA, the Abuses of Anti-Terrorism, and the Strategy of Transparency,* 11 LEWIS & CLARK L. REV. 1141 (2007); Bradley Pack, *FOIA Frustration: Access to Government Records Under the Bush Administration,* 46 ARIZ. L. R. 815 (2004).

[147]*See, e.g.,* David Cuillier, *Public Support for Press Access Declines as Personal Privacy Concerns Increase,* 25 NEWSPAPER RES. J. 95 (2007) (finding a correlation between fear of privacy invasion and reduced support for open records); Wendell Cochran & Jonathan Katz, FOIA Requests Increasingly Denied for Privacy, not Security, Grounds, paper presented at Investigative Reporters and Editors national conference, June 2003, Washington, D.C.

[148]*See, e.g.,* Aaron Mackey, *In Wake of Journal News Publishing Gun Permit Holder Maps, Nation Sees Push to Limit Access to Gun Records,* 37 NEWS MEDIA & L. 4 (2014). (The National Rifle Association has successfully lobbied to close concealed weapon per-

Further, the reduction of news organizations' resources today might have Cross rolling in his grave, based on his perception of a relatively apathetic press in 1953. For example, Cross wrote that newspapers had more success obtaining information through "sugar" of relationship-building and source development, rather than the "vinegar" of legal compulsion.[149] He encouraged journalists to continue this approach – to use diplomacy and public shaming rather than the law, when possible. Today, newsroom staffs have been slashed,[150] making it more difficult for journalists to find the time to develop sources and pursue public record requests.[151]

Cross also noted that news organizations were successful when they sued for access, and he encouraged them to embark on more litigation to combat growing secrecy. Today, however, news editors say their organizations are less likely to sue for public records than they were ten years ago.[152] Unless other constituencies, such as non-profit groups, rise up to fill the gaps left by a hamstrung press, freedom of information could be at risk.

Cross ultimately urged Congress to take action:

> In a democracy such a state of affairs is a continuing challenge to public and press. Its growth has gone unchallenged too long. It stems largely from the philosophy of an official cult of secrecy.... The condition cries aloud for abatement. Congress is the primary source for relief... The time is ripe for an end to ineffectual sputtering about executive refusals of access to official records and for Congress to begin exercising effectually

mits in most states); Relly & Schwalbe, *supra* note 20 (business interests lobbying to make records secret).

[149] CROSS, *supra* note 1, at 5.

[150] The news industry in 2015 suffered the worst year since the 2008 recession, with a 7% drop in newspaper circulation, an 8% decline in advertising, and a 10% reduction in staffing, according to the Pew Research Center State of the Media 2016, *available at* http://www.journalism.org/2016/06/15/state-of-the-news-media-2016/ (last visited July 13, 2016). Daily newspapers supported 32,900 full-time newsroom employees in 2015, down from a high of 56,900 in 1990. *See* American Society of News Editors Newsroom Employment Diversity Survey, *available at* http://asne.org/content.asp?pl=140&sl=129&contentid=129 (last visited July 13, 2016).

[151] *See* David Cuillier, Pressed for Time: U.S. Journalists' Use of Public Records During Economic Crisis, paper presented at the Global Conference on Transparency Research, May 19, 2011, Newark, N.J. (finding that half of U.S. journalists have never submitted a federal FOIA request, a quarter said they don't have time, a third that they don't know how, and a third perceive that their companies are less likely to sue for records than in past two years).

[152] Knight Foundation survey, *supra* note 93.

> its function to legislate freedom of information for itself, the public, and the press.[153]

Congress listened to Cross, and thirteen years later enacted such relief through the Freedom of Information Act.

Conclusion

In the fifty years since Congress passed FOIA, the legal landscape has matured and become more articulated through statute and court interpretation. This has resulted in benefits and drawbacks for journalists and the public seeking information about their government. Despite the more detailed articulation of access rights in the United States, requesters still call for more transparency and lament what they perceive to be a general movement toward secrecy, as Cross did in 1953.[154]

Perhaps transparency and secrecy are cyclical, rising and falling due to societal pressures and global events. Patrice McDermott, director of Openthegovernment.org, suggests that transparency peaked by the early 1990s, calling the Bill Clinton administration the "golden age" of transparency.[155] While there were indications of increasing secrecy, the general presumption was openness and the Internet was fueling a feeling of transparency. That changed quickly, McDermott wrote, when George W. Bush came to power.[156]

Or, perhaps the tussle between transparency and secrecy is eternal. Mitchell Pearlman, director and counsel for the Connecticut Freedom of Information Committee from 1975 to 2005, noted the nature of the cycles of government transparency and the ongoing struggle that societies will need to work through:

> I believe that the fight for Freedom of Information will continue well into the future. Where and when the pendulum swings toward transparency, the fight will take on an offensive posture; where and when the pendulum swings in the other direction, the battle likely will be a defensive one ...

---

153 Cross, *supra* note 1, at 246.

154 *See, e.g., FOIA at Fifty: Has the Sunshine Law's Promise Been Fulfilled? Hearing before the S. Comm. On the Judiciary,* 114th Cong. (2016), *available at* http://www.judiciary.senate.gov/meetings/foia-at-fifty-has-the-sunshine-laws-promise-been-fulfilled (last visited July 13, 2016) (delineating testimony by panelists, including the author, discussing continued secrecy and the need for further fixes to FOIA).

155 Patrice McDermott, Who Needs to Know? The State of Public Access to Federal Government Information 195 (2007).

156 *Id.*

> The fight for Freedom of Information will end only with the birth of a utopian society – a highly unlikely event, at least within my projected lifetime. If Utopia itself is unattainable, we nonetheless can strive to make society 'a more perfect union' between government and governed.[157]

Ultimately, while problems still exist and the struggle continues for maintaining open, accountable government, evidence from this study suggests that the people's right to know is, overall, stronger today than it was in 1953. More research needs to be done to identify the trajectory in transparency's evolution, where and when it rises and falls, and the influences on freedom of information that can guide policy makers today and in the future. The key, it seems, is to remain vigilant in moving ahead, as Cross emphasized:

> Citizens of a self-governing society must have the legal right to examine and investigate the conduct of its affairs, subject only to those limitations imposed by the most urgent public necessity. To that end they must have the right to simple, speedy enforcement procedure geared to cope with the dynamic expansion of government activity. These rights must be elevated to a position of the highest sanction if the people are to enter into full enjoyment of their right to know. Freedom of information is the very foundation for all those freedoms that the First Amendment of our Constitution was intended to guarantee.[158]

---

[157] MITCHELL W. PEARLMAN, PIERCING THE VEIL OF SECRECY: LESSONS IN THE FIGHT FOR FREEDOM OF INFORMATION 136 (2010).

[158] CROSS, *supra* note 1, at xiii-xiv.

The Fiftieth Anniversary of the Freedom of Information Act: How it Measures up Against International Standards and Other Laws

Toby Mendel

When the United States adopted its Freedom of Information Act in 1966, it was the third country in the world to put in place such a groundbreaking democratic mechanism for ensuring public access to the information held by government. As such, it was, by definition, a global leader in this area. Fifty years later, however, according to the internationally recognized tool for assessing legal frameworks for what has come to be known as the right to information, or RTI, the RTI Rating, the United States FOIA languishes in the fifty-first position globally. This article describes the way the RTI Rating works and analyses the strengths and weaknesses of the FOIA according to the rating. In some cases, these weaknesses appear to be derived, at least in part, from the age of the FOIA, and a correlation can be found between the performance of the United States law and other older laws. In other cases, further study is needed to identify the causes of the weaknesses.

This year marks the fiftieth anniversary of the adoption of the United States Freedom of Information Act.[1] This type of law – which grants individuals the right of access to information held by public authorities – has come to be known globally as a "right to information," or RTI law, in light of the fact that the right it guarantees is now recognized internationally as a human right, guaranteed as part of the broader right to freedom of expression.[2] The United States was the third country in the world to adopt such a law, following Sweden (1766, so that it is celebrating the 250th anniversary of its law this year) and Finland (1951).

---

[1]Freedom of Information Act, 5 U.S.C. §552 (2012).
[2]*See infra* notes 17, 18, 19 and accompanying text.

Twenty-five years after the FOIA was adopted – in 1991 – only fourteen countries had adopted such laws, although the number has grown rapidly since then and, as of June 30, 2016, stood at 108 national laws (and a far greater number of sub-national laws) globally.[3]

As an early adopter, and a country that has introduced a significant number of amendments to its law, one might assume that the United States would be a leader in this area. According to the RTI Rating,[4] the leading global methodology for measuring the strength of the legal framework for RTI,[5] that assumption is wrong. Indeed, the rating puts the United States in a tie for fifty-first position globally, alongside Australia, Belize, Honduras and Romania, just about the middle point of all countries with such laws.[6] Furthermore, the rating only credits the United States FOIA with eighty-three points out of a possible 150, or less than 55%, far less than top-scoring Serbia, with 135 points (90%).[7]

This article describes the RTI Rating and the international and comparative standards from which it was developed and then looks at areas where the United States FOIA does comparatively better or less well, putting forward some theories to explain its performance. An initial observation is that the United States at least does better than a number of established democracies, which account for exactly one-half of both the bottom ten and bottom twenty countries on the rating and which are (from the bottom): Austria, Liechtenstein, Germany, Italy,[8] Belgium, Iceland, France, Denmark, Greece and Japan. Furthermore, not a single Western democracy makes it onto the top-twenty list, with Finland at the top of this group, in twenty-second position globally.

[3]*See Global Right to Information, Country Data*, https://www.rti-rating.org/country-data. The data in this article are taken from the rating as it stood on June 30, 2016, and any changes since then are not reflected herein.

[4]RTI RATING, https://www.rti-rating.org.

[5]It should be stressed that the rating only measures the strength of the legal framework for RTI and not the quality of implementation of the rules. There are cases of countries with relatively weak laws which still achieve fairly high degrees of transparency, while a few countries with strong laws have done almost nothing to implement them. *See* Ethiopia: Article 19 Submission to the UN Universal Periodic Review of Ethiopia, Sept. 16, 2013, *available at* https://www.article19.org/resources.php/resource/37245/en/ethiopia:-article-19-submission-to-the-un-universal-periodic-review-of-ethiopia.

[6]Note that, as of June 30, 2016, only 103 countries had been assessed on the rating, and with ratings for five other laws still being completed.

[7]The high Serbia score, along with high scores of a few other countries at the top of the rating, suggests that the standards the rating relies on are not unrealistically strict or idealistic.

[8]A new law came into force in Italy in late June 2016, but the score on the RTI Rating has not yet been updated.

Sweden, for its part, sits a little bit ahead of the United States, in forty-first position with ninety-two points.

Age of the legislation – in the sense of the time since it was first adopted[9] – seems to have something to do with performance. None of the countries in the top twenty positions in the RTI Rating were adopted before 2000, while nine of the ten Western laws in the bottom twenty countries were adopted before 2000 (Germany, 2005, is the exception). And there are fairly plausible explanations for this. As elaborated below,[10] the development of clear international standards in this area has almost all taken place since 2000, and these standards have, in turn, provided a template or at least guidance for newer legislation. Recognition as a human right internationally has also come about since 2000, and that again has contributed to pressure for the development of stronger national legislation. Later laws have the advantage of building on the successes and failures of earlier laws. And cross-cutting these themes is the fact that while legislation can always be amended, there are usually barriers to this – at least in terms of time and legislative attention but there are often also more active forms of opposition such as resistance from the bureaucracy – and it is easier to incorporate new ideas into legislation from scratch or by design than to retrofit them into older legislation.

But there also may be a more structural element to the overall weak performance of Western democracies. Although Western democracies have been in the forefront of the development and recognition of many human rights, this has not been the case with the right to information. Indeed, it is significant that in cases dating back to 1985, the European Court of Human Rights consistently refused to recognize the right, and did so only in 2009, following recognition by the Inter-American Court of Human Rights in 2006.[11] One possible reason which has been identified for this is that access to information is viewed in the West primarily as a governance reform, rather than as giving effect to a human right, which is a more dominant view in at least some other countries.[12] This, in turn, has a profound affect on the political narrative and dynamics around both the development and implementation of the legislation.

---

[9]As opposed to the time since the most recent set of amendments.

[10]*See infra* notes 17-26 and accompanying text.

[11]*See infra* note 17.

[12]*See* TOBY MENDEL, RIGHT TO INFORMATION: RECENT SPREAD OF RTI LEGISLATION 4 (2014), *available at* http://siteresources.worldbank.org/PUBLICSECTORANDGOVERNANCE/Resources/285741-1343934891414/8787489-1344020463266/8788935-1399321576201/Recent-Spread-of-RTI-Legislation.pdf.

The RTI Rating

The RTI Rating was developed by two civil society organizations – the Centre for Law and Democracy[13] and Access Info Europe[14] – which are recognized globally for their expertise on the right to information. Sixty-one indicators, according to which points are awarded for specific RTI legal qualities or attributes, lie at the heart of the RTI Rating methodology. The indicators are based on an analysis of a wide range of international standards relating to the right to information, as well as a comparative study of numerous right to information laws from around the world.

The standards the RTI Rating sets for RTI laws, or the attributes which are credited with points, which are reflected in the indicators, are drawn from those international standards and comparative practice. A core idea behind the rating is that it is rooted in international human rights law, as opposed to simply an assessment of good or better practice. To this extent, the rating standards can claim to be legally binding on states. In most cases, the standards are based on a principled analysis of formally binding standards, but in a few cases – such as the cut-offs for awarding points for the time limits for responding to requests – reasonable but ultimately discretionary standards were adopted.

Although CLD and AIE led the process, an advisory council, which included members from countries around the world, was closely involved in the process and commented on successive drafts until the final version was essentially adopted by consensus. During the development phase, the indicators were applied to a representative sample of countries to assess whether they were workable and appeared to deliver sensible outcomes, and they were then revised to take into account the results.

The indicators are grouped into seven higher-order categories, namely: Right of Access, Scope, Requesting Procedures, Exceptions and Refusals, Appeals, Sanctions and Protections, and Promotional Measures. The total score allocated to the four central categories – Scope, Requesting Procedures, Exceptions and Refusals, and Appeals – is set at thirty points each, on the basis that these represent roughly equivalent general attributes of strong RTI laws, while the remaining three categories – Right of Access, Sanctions and Protections, and Promotional Measures – are together allocated another thirty points, or six,

[13]Centre for Law and Democracy, http://www.law-democracy.org/live/.

[14]Access Info Europe, https://www.access-info.org.

eight and sixteen points, respectively, giving an overall total of 150 points.

A large majority of the indicators, fifty-two out of sixty-one, are worth a maximum of two points, while the other nine are allocated scores of up to ten points. The thinking here was to avoid trying to super-fine-tune scoring – which is misleading and may give the wrong impression as to the claims the authors are implicitly making regarding the level of precision of the tool, since more refined scoring suggests a greater level of precision – and instead aim to break down the qualities of laws into roughly equal granular attributes. At the same time, it would have been artificial to try to reduce all of the characteristics assessed by the indicators to the same small size. An example is the subject matter of different exceptions (or the types of interests they protect, such as national security or privacy), measured by Indicator 29, which is allocated a maximum of ten points.

Points are allocated by indicator, depending on how well the legal framework delivers the indicator, in accordance with a standardized scoring tool, which aims to ensure that points are allocated consistently across different countries and legal systems. In all but two cases, points are allocated on a positive basis (that is, points are awarded where a characteristic is present), but for the indicators on the subject matter of exceptions and whether exceptions are harm tested points are allocated on a negative basis (that is, countries are awarded, respectively, ten and four points, and then a point is deducted for each exception the subject matter of which is not recognized as legitimate under international law or which does not incorporate a harm test).

Although the primary indicators have not been updated since the tool was launched on September 28, 2011 (International Right to Know Day),[15] the scoring tool has been tweaked and updated over time. A particular challenge has been to ensure fair and yet fully standardized application of the methodology across different legal and access to information systems, but for the most part challenges in this area have been addressed in ways which have generally been deemed to be satisfactory.

The way the methodology is applied has been designed with the dual objectives of robust standardization and accuracy of assessment as the primary goals. To promote the former, assessments are closely overseen

[15]For more information about International Right to Know Day, *see* http://foiadvocates.net/?page_id=10255. In November 2015, UNESCO adopted a declaration formally recognizing the same day as International Day for Universal Access to Information. For more information, *see* http://www.opengovpartnership.org/blog/blog-editor/2015/11/25/international-day-universal-access-information-new-opportunity-advance.

by researchers at CLD and AIE,[16] while the latter is promoted through both careful attention to detail and having local experts review initial assessments to identify any gaps or misinterpretations in the appreciation of the local legal framework. The RTI Rating is applied on a continuous basis as new countries adopt or amend their RTI laws and/or regulations, and an attempt is made as far as possible to keep up with other developments, such as jurisprudence which reaches the level of impacting on an Indicator. The support of local experts is of course essential for this.

International Sources for the RTI Rating

There are two main strands to the international sources for the RTI Rating. The first is application of the standards and principles relating to freedom of expression to the right to information. This, in turn, rests on the progressive recognition that the right to information is protected as part of the wider right to freedom of expression under international law. This recognition has become increasingly entrenched, especially in the five years between 2006 and 2011, and it is now very widely accepted.

Key milestones in the process were the September 2006 Inter-American Court of Human Rights case of *Claude Reyes and Others v. Chile*,[17] the April 2009 European Court of Human Rights case of *Társaság A Szabadságjogokért v. Hungary*,[18] and the September 2011 General Comment No. 34 of the United Nations Human Rights Committee.[19] In the *Reyes* case, the Inter-American Court of Human Rights held explicitly that the right to freedom of expression, as enshrined in

[16]Various systems were also put in place to ensure standardization across the two organizations.

[17]Sept. 19, 2006, Series C, No. 151, *available at* http://www.corteidh.or.cr/docs/casos/articulos/seriec_151_ing.doc.

[18]Apr. 14, 2009, Application No. 37374/05. Interestingly, the respondent State in the case, Hungary, did not even contest the claim that the guarantee of freedom of expression also included the right to information, and instead limited itself to arguing that the information in question fell within the scope of the exceptions to this right (i.e. that the refusal to provide it was a legitimate restriction on freedom of expression).

[19]General Comment No. 34, Sept. 12, 2011, CCPR/C/GC/34, *available at* http://tbinternet.ohchr.org/_layouts/treatybodyexternal/TBSearch.aspx?Lang = en&TreatyID = 8&DocTypeID = 11. The committee is the body tasked with promoting the implementation of the rights set out in the International Covenant on Civil and Political Rights, UN General Assembly Resolution 2200 A (XXI), adopted Dec. 16, 1966, entered into force Mar. 23, 1976.

Article 13 of the American Convention on Human Rights,[20] included a right to access information held by public authorities (that is, the right to information). The European Court came to a similar conclusion in the *Társaság A Szabadságjogokért* case,[21] while in General Comment No. 34 the U.N. Human Rights Committee stated simply, with reference to Article 19 of the International Covenant on Civil and Political Rights, or ICCPR,[22] also guaranteeing freedom of expression: "Article 19, paragraph 2 embraces a right of access to information held by public bodies."[23]

In the *Reyes* case, the Inter-American Court of Human Rights discussed in some detail the legitimate scope of exceptions to the right, making it clear that its previous jurisprudence relating to restrictions on freedom of expression applied, *mutatis mutandis*, to the right to information.[24] It is relatively simple to extrapolate from this, and indeed directly from general principles of law, that recognition of the right to information as a component of the right to freedom of expression brings into play in respect of the former the full gamut of general principles and standards relating to the latter insofar as they are relevant and applicable. As regards exceptions to the right of access, under international law, to be legitimate, a restriction on freedom of expression (and so an exception to the right to information) must be prescribed by law, serve one of the interests listed in Article 19(3) of the ICCPR which are deemed to be sufficiently important to warrant limiting freedom of expression, and be necessary for the protection of that interest.[25] International law also imposes clear positive obligations on states to give effect to the right to freedom of expression and, by implication, the right to information.[26]

A number of the standards reflected in the RTI Rating indicators are drawn from a principled analysis of international standards, in

[20]Adopted at San José, Costa Rica, Nov. 22, 1969, O.A.S. Treaty Series No. 36, entered into force July 18, 1978.

[21]Based on Article 10 of the European Convention on Human Rights, E.T.S. No. 5, adopted Nov. 4, 1950, entered into force Sept. 3, 1953.

[22]*See* General Comment No 34, *supra* note 19.

[23]Claude Ryes and Others v. Chile, Sept. 19, 2006, at paras. 18–19.

[24]Sept. 19, 2006, Series C, No. 151, *available at* http://www.corteidh.or.cr/docs/casos/articulos/seriec_151_ing.doc, paras. 88-91.

[25]*See* General Comment No. 34, *supra* note 19, para. 22. *See also* Mukong v. Cameroon, July 21, 1994, Communication No.458/1991, at para.9.7 (UN Human Rights Committee); Sunday Times v. United Kingdom, Apr. 26, 1979, Application No. 6538/74 (European Court of Human Rights).

[26]*See* Toby Mendel, Restricting Freedom of Expression: Standards and Principles Background Paper for Meetings Hosted by the UN Special Rapporteur on Freedom of Opinion and Expression 5 (2010), *available at* http://www.law-democracy.org/live/wp-content/uploads/2012/08/Paper-on-Restrictions.10.03.22.rev_.pdf.

some cases as interpreted in light of better comparative practice. It is well established that restrictions on freedom of expression, even where some restriction is warranted to protect a legitimate interest, may not be overbroad in the sense of prohibiting speech (or access to information) beyond where this would cause harm,[27] and must employ the least intrusive means available for protecting the legitimate interest.[28] The flip side of this – less well articulated in the jurisprudence but clear from a logical extrapolation of principles – is the duty of states to give effect to their positive obligations in a, let us say "most enabling" manner, subject to reasonable limitations on resources and effort. Comparative practice on the part of other states is invaluable, among other things because it has been tested in practice, means of illustrating the specific modalities of all of these required characteristics (that is, narrowest scope of exceptions, least intrusive means of protecting an interest and most enabling manner of discharging positive obligations).

For example, there are obvious right-to-information benefits to applicants of being issued with a receipt upon lodging a request for information. At the same time, this imposes a limited burden on public authorities. It is also a requirement in the laws of many countries. As a result, the rating accepts that this is a minimum RTI standard and includes it in Indicator 18. General principles of human rights law – for example that all state actors are bound by that state's human rights obligations – underpin other standards in the rating – in that case, the rules on scope and, in particular, the need to extend the right to all three branches of government. This is supported by the fact that many states effectively apply their right to information laws to all branches of government, apparently without placing undue strain on public resources or generating other negative impacts.

Relying on comparative analysis for an exercise like this brings with it a risk of offending against human rights principles which allow for local tailoring, at least in terms of the means of implementation, of international standards. However, given the nature of the right to information, and the rather extensive judicial interpretation of international guarantees of freedom of expression, the extent to which local tailoring of standards is justifiable is relatively clear. These sources make it clear that there is relatively little need or justification for this, at

[27]*See* Shelton v. Tucker, 364 U.S. 479, 488 (1960); R. v. Oakes, [1986] 1 SCR 103, pp. 138-39 (Supreme Court of Canada).

[28]As the Inter-American Court of Human Rights stated in *Compulsory Membership in an Association Prescribed by Law for the Practice of Journalism*, Advisory Opinion OC-5/85, Nov. 13, 1985, Series A, No. 5, para. 46: "Hence if there are various options to achieve this objective, that which least restricts the right protected must be selected."

least in terms of general standards, with the exception of the issue of institutional structures. For example, it is undisputed that it is legitimate to posit privacy as an exception to the right of access. While local cultural understandings of what constitutes privacy vary, this does not impact on the RTI Rating, which limits itself to recognizing privacy as a legitimate exception to the right of access (and not probing into the specific content of this). On the other hand, the peculiar exception in the U.S. FOIA in favor of "geological and geophysical information and data, including maps, concerning wells"[29] is not deemed by the RTI Rating to be legitimate because it is not included in the laws of other countries, this has not caused any harm which might justify the exception, and there are no particular cultural or other special characteristics of the situation in the United States which would justify the exception.

Only a handful of cases on the right to information have been decided by international courts and that was even more true in 2011 when the current indicators for the RTI Rating were developed.[30] However, this does not mean that the indicators were drawn exclusively from a principled analysis of freedom of expression standards in the context of the right to information, as interpreted using the practical filter of better national practice. In addition to this, as the second strand of international sources, the Indicators drew on a strong body of what might be called soft law standards relating to the right to information, which had started to be put in place well before even the first instance of judicial recognition of the right, a process which has continued since that time.

There were a few early standard-setting statements about the right to information, of which perhaps the earliest was the adoption, in 1981, by the Committee of Ministers of the Council of Europe, of Recommendation No. R(81)19 on Access to Information Held by Public Authorities.[31] However, these very early statements were not presented as rights-based statements, and so do not provide a solid basis for the RTI

[29] Freedom of Information Act, 5 U.S.C. §552(b)(9)(2012).

[30] In addition to the cases mentioned, the European Court of Human Rights had also decided *Kenedi v. Hungary*, May 26, 2009, Application No. 31475/05 by that time. It has decided a few more cases since then. *See, e.g.*, Österreichische Vereinigung zur Erhaltung, Stärkung und Schaffung eines wirtschaftlich gesunden land- und forstwirtschaftlichen Grundbesitzes v. Austria, Nov. 28, 2013, Application No. 39534/07.

[31] Nov. 25, 1981, *available at* https://wcd.coe.int/com.instranet.InstraServlet?command=com.instranet.CmdBlobGet&InstranetImage=600652&SecMode=1&DocId=673752&Usage=2. *See also* statements adopted at the 1980 Barbados meeting of the Law Ministers of the Commonwealth, *quoted in* Promoting Open Government: Commonwealth Principles and Guidelines on the Right to Know, background paper for the Commonwealth Expert Group Meeting on the Right to Know and the Promotion of Democracy and Development, London, Mar. 30-31, 1999, *available at*

Rating Indicators which, as noted above, are intended to be rooted in international human rights standards.

Some of the earliest rights-based statements about the right to information came in the annual reports of the U.N. Special Rapporteur on Freedom of Opinion and Expression, whose mandate is formally limited in scope to human rights.[32] In his 1998 Annual Report to the Human Rights Commission, for example, the Special Rapporteur stated: "[T]he right to seek, receive and impart information imposes a positive obligation on States to ensure access to information, particularly with regard to information held by Government in all types of storage and retrieval systems."[33] The U.N. Special Rapporteur substantially expanded his commentary on this subject in his 2000 Annual Report[34] and has provided further elaborations in a number of subsequent reports. The U.N. Special Rapporteur's counterparts – the Organization for Security and Co-operation in Europe Representative on Freedom of the Media, the Organization of American States Special Rapporteur on Freedom of Expression, and the African Commission on Human and Peoples' Rights Special Rapporteur on Freedom of Expression and Access to Information – have also often included commentary on the right to information in their reports.[35]

These special international mandates on freedom of expression have since 1999 adopted a Joint Declaration each year on a different freedom of expression issue. The first Joint Declaration was general in nature, and included the following statement about the right to information: "Implicit in freedom of expression is the public's right to open access to information and to know what governments are doing on their behalf, without which truth would languish and people's participation in government would remain fragmented."[36]

---

http://www.humanrightsinitiative.org/programs/ai/rti/international/cw_standards/commonwealth_expert_grp_on_the_rti_99-03-00.pdf.

[32]The mandate of the Special Rapporteur was originally set out in United Nations Commission on Human Rights Resolution 1993/45, Mar. 5, 1993, para. 11., http://ap.ohchr.org/documents/E/CHR/resolutions/E-CN_4-RES-1993-45.doc. If he or she does address an issue, that signifies his or her view that it falls within the mandate of the office, which is limited to topics relating to the right to freedom of expression.

[33]Report of the Special Rapporteur, Promotion and Protection of the Right to Freedom of Opinion and Expression, UN Doc. E/CN.4/1998/40, Jan. 28, 1998, para. 14, *available at* https://documents-dds-ny.un.org/doc/UNDOC/GEN/G98/103/12/PDF/G9810312.pdf?OpenElement.

[34]Report of the Special Rapporteur, *Promotion and Protection of the Right to Freedom of Opinion and Expression*, UN Doc. E/CN.4/2000/63, Jan. 18, 2000, para. 42.

[35]*See, e.g.*, the 1999 Report of the OAS Special Rapporteur on Freedom of Expression, at 29-33, http://www.oas.org/es/cidh/expresion/showarticle.asp?artID = 135&lID = 1.

[36]Adopted Nov. 26, 1999. All of the Joint Declarations are *available at* http://www.osce.org/fom/66176.

The mandates provided more detailed statements on the nature of the right to information in their Joint Declarations of 2004,[37] 2006[38] and 2010.[39]

Other important sources of right to information standards are the declarations on freedom of expression adopted in 2000 by the Inter-American Commission on Human Rights[40] and in 2002 by the African Commission on Human and Peoples' Rights.[41] Both declarations include important statements about standards regarding the right to information, based on its status as an element of the right to freedom of expression.

In addition, in 2002, the Committee of Ministers of the Council of Europe adopted Recommendation No. R(2002)2 on Access to Official Documents,[42] which is specifically dedicated to the right to information and contains more detailed standards than the general declarations adopted in the Americas and Africa. In 2008, however, the Americas followed suit when the Inter-American Juridical Committee adopted a progressive set of Principles on the Right of Access to Information.[43]

In both the Americas and Africa, official human rights bodies have also adopted model laws on the right to information. In the Americas, a Model Inter-American Law on Access to Information was prepared by the Department of International Law of the Secretariat for Legal Affairs of the OAS, and welcomed in a resolution of the OAS General Assembly,[44] while the African Commission on Human and Peoples' Rights adopted the Model Law on Access to Information for Africa in 2013.[45] Although these are intended more to provide guidance and support to countries which are considering the adoption or amendment of right to information legislation, they also provide some insight into what are considered to be minimum standards regarding these rights.

[37]*Id.* adopted Dec. 6, 2004.

[38]*Id.* adopted Dec. 19, 2006.

[39]*Id.* adopted 3 Feb. 3, 2010.

[40]The Inter-American Declaration of Principles on Freedom of Expression, 108th Regular Session, Oct. 19, 2000, http://www.iachr.org/declaration.htm.

[41]The Declaration of Principles on Freedom of Expression in Africa, 32d Ordinary Session of the African Commission on Human and Peoples' Rights, Oct. 17-23, 2002, Banjul, The Gambia, http://www.achpr.org/english/declarations/declaration_freedom_exp_en.html.

[42]Adopted Feb. 21, 2002, *available at* http://www.right2info.org/resources/publications/instruments-and-standards/coe_rec_ati_en_2002.

[43]Adopted at its 73d Regular Session, Aug. 7, 2008 in Rio de Janeiro, Brazil, OAS/Ser.Q, CJI/RES.147 (LXXIII-O/08), *available at* http://www.oas.org/cji/eng/CJI-RES_147_LXXIII-O-08_eng.pdf.

[44]AG/RES. 2607 (XL-O/10), June 8, 2010, *available at* http://www.oas.org/en/sla/dil/docs/AG-RES_2607-2010_eng.pdf.

[45]*Available at* http://www.achpr.org/files/news/2013/04/d84/model_law.pdf.

Table 1
Scores of the United States FOIA on the RTI Rating

Section	Max Points	Score	Percentage
1. Right of Access	6	2	33
2. Scope	30	18	60
3. Requesting Procedures	30	16	53
4. Exceptions and Refusals	30	17	57
5. Appeals	30	14	47
6. Sanctions and Protections	8	4	50
7. Promotional Measures	16	12	75
Total Score	150	83	55

Finally, within Europe, a formal legal treaty, the Council of Europe Convention on Access to Official Documents, was adopted in 2009.[46] Although not yet in force,[47] the Convention does again provide useful evidence of what at least European States consider to be minimum standards in this area. All of these sources were relied upon to help develop the Indicators for the RTI Rating.[48]

Application of the RTI Rating to the United States FOIA

The scores of the United States FOIA, broken down by category, are set out in Table 1. Formally, these scores do not represent an assessment only of the FOIA but of the wider legal framework for access to information. In some cases, RTI Rating indicators explicitly refer to other laws, such as Indicator 1, which asks whether the right to information is constitutionally protected. In all cases, a formal legal rule or even binding policy which, in fact, delivers the quality described in an indicator will garner the points for the country, regardless of whether it is found within or under the RTI law or elsewhere.

Table 1 makes it clear that the worst performing area in the United States is Right of Access, which, along with Appeals, are the two categories where the score drops below 50%. However, if we exclude the top and bottom performing categories (the former being promotional

[46]CETS No. 205, opened for ratification June 18, 2009, not yet in force, http://www.coe.int/en/web/conventions/full-list/-/conventions/treaty/205.

[47]According to Article 16 of the Convention, it will enter into force three months after receiving the tenth ratification. As of June 24, 2016, eight states had ratified the convention.

[48]Although the African Model Law had not yet formally been adopted by the time the rating was first launched, work on it had already started by then.

measures, where the FOIA does relatively better), the other scores fall within the reasonably narrow range of 47% to 60%.

Right of Access

The United States gets no points on two of the three indicators in this category of the RTI Rating and two points on Indicator 2, which asks whether the right has clearly been recognized in law. The FOIA does not include a reference to its wider benefits or provide any interpretive guidance, so it gets no points for Indicator 3, which measures these qualities. An explicit constitutional guarantee of this right clearly meets the standards of Indicator 1.[49] According to some sources, nearly sixty countries include explicit guarantees of the right to information in their constitutions.[50] This does not include the many countries around the world, mostly from among civil law countries, which incorporate international law and/or international human rights law directly into their national legal systems. While such provisions are not given proper legal effect in many countries, this is not the case everywhere. In Europe, for example, the courts of many countries treat European Court of Human Rights decisions as formally binding, thereby effectively incorporating the guarantee of the right to information from that system into national law. In the United States, however, there is no explicit guarantee of the right to information in the Constitution and nor is any international guarantee incorporated into United States law in the overriding (constitutional) sense, as required by Indicator 1.

This indicator also accepts a constitutional interpretation by a superior court holding that the right to information is included within or covered by another constitutionally protected right. Leading courts in a number of countries have interpreted constitutional guarantees – free expression, for example – to include the right to information.[51] However, the language of the First Amendment to the United States Constitution does not easily lead itself to such an interpretation, being cast in the negative term of prohibiting the government from passing laws restricting free speech. And, in practice, the Supreme Court of the United States has held that the guarantee of freedom of speech in the

---

[49]Technically, the indicator is looking for whether the legal framework recognizes a "fundamental right of access to information."

[50]*See* Right2Info, Constitutional Protections, http://www.right2info.org/constitutional-protections.

[51]*See, e.g.*, Ontario (Public Safety and Security) v. Criminal Lawyers' Association, 2010 SCC 23, June 17, 2010 (Supreme Court of Canada), *available at* http://www.canlii.org/en/ca/scc/doc/2010/2010scc23/2010scc23.html.

first Amendment does not mandate "a right to access government information or sources of information within government's control."[52]

Scope

This category assesses the scope of the rules in terms of three metrics: who may make a request for information, what information is covered, and what public authorities (or agencies to use the term in the United States FOIA) are covered. The act does very well in terms of the first two metrics, only losing one point out of a possible eight.[53]

The situation is different in terms of the scope of the act in terms of public authorities, where it garners only one-half of the twenty-two points. The main losses come because the act is limited in scope to the executive branch of government, along with state-owned enterprises and regulatory bodies. While it does very well in these areas, fully eight points are lost for lack of coverage of the legislative or judicial branches of government, along with two more for a failure to cover private bodies that operate with significant public funding or that undertake a public function.

The obligation to apply the right to information to all three branches of government flows quite clearly from recognition of the right to information as a human right. As the U.N. Human Rights Committee stated in General Comment No. 31:

> The obligations of the Covenant in general and article 2 in particular [requiring States to respect and to give effect to rights] are binding on every State Party as a whole. All branches of government (executive, legislative and judicial), and other public or governmental authorities, at whatever level - national, regional or local – are in a position to engage the responsibility of the State Party.[54]

Reflecting this, nine of the top ten scoring countries on the rating got the full eight points for coverage of the legislative and judicial branches of government (which are measured by Indicators 8 and 9), while one (Mexico in both cases) received two out of four points for each branch.

[52]Houchins v. KQED, Inc., 438 U.S. 1, 15 (1978).

[53]This is because the extent to which public authorities must compile information from different documents in response to a request is not entirely clear.

[54]General Comment No. 31, May 26, 2004, CCPR/C/21/Rev.1/Add. 13, paragraph 4, *available at* http://tbinternet.ohchr.org/_layouts/treatybodyexternal/TBSearch.aspx?Lang = en&TreatyID = 8&DocTypeID = 11.

Table 2
Scores of Different Groups of Countries for Coverage of the Legislative and Judicial Branches

Legislative/Judicial	No points	1 point	2 points	3 points	4 points
Earliest Laws	7/5	1/3	0/0	0/0	2/2
Latest Laws	1/1	1/1	0/1	1/0	7/7
Best Laws	0/0	0/0	1/1	0/0	9/9

The date the right-to-information law was adopted would appear to play a role here, with only two of the earliest ten laws scoring more than one point for either branch (these being Sweden and Finland, which both scored full points for both branches). In contrast, fully seven of the ten countries with the most recent laws[55] scored full points for both the legislative and judicial branches, with scores ranging from zero to three for the other three countries. These results are presented in Table 2.

There may also be a difference here between established Western democracies where, as noted previously, the human rights status of access to information is not always fully appreciated, and countries in some other regions of the world. It is perhaps significant that the worst performer in this area among the countries with the latest laws is Spain, with only one point for both branches, which is also the only Western democracy in that cohort.[56] More research on this issue is needed before a firmer conclusion can be drawn.

The top-scoring countries also do very well in terms of coverage of private bodies that operate with public funding or that undertake public functions, with eight of the ten scoring the full two points here and the other two obtaining one point. Older laws do comparatively better here than in relation to branches of government, albeit with only one (Denmark) getting two points but with another six getting one point (leaving only two of the ten – Australia and Canada – alongside the United States with no points here).

Requesting Procedures

This is perhaps the category where the standards of the RTI Rating represent the greatest extrapolation of the principle of the most

[55]As included on the RTI Rating at the time this article was written. Due to the time it takes to assess new laws, and in some cases delays due to translation, the most recent laws are not always available on the rating.

[56]Although Sierra Leone only garnered two points for these two indicators.

enabling approach towards discharging positive obligations. At one level, it is clear that user-friendly procedures are key to the practical success of an RTI law, and there is ample evidence of the problems that unfriendly or unduly flexible procedural rules can cause. This has also been chronicled in the United States, for example in relation to delays in responding to requests[57] and fees.[58] At the same time, it is hard to describe all the standards reflected in the indicators in this category as strict human rights obligations. For example, Indicator 22 allocates one point for time limits of twenty or fewer working days and two points for limits of ten or fewer days. Obviously, at some level these are arbitrary cut-offs, although there is a logic to them. Overall, it is clear that an RTI law simply cannot function well absent strong procedural rules governing the making and processing of requests.

The soft law standards noted above provide some assistance here as to appropriate procedural rules for RTI laws. A number of standards refer to general principles governing procedures. For example, the 2004 Joint Declaration of the special international mandates on freedom of expression calls for procedures to "be simple, rapid and free or low-cost."[59] The Principles on the Right of Access to Information adopted by Inter-American Juridical Committee call generally for "clear, fair, non-discriminatory and simple rules" for processing requests. Principle 5 goes on to stipulate that these should include "clear and reasonable timelines, provision for assistance to be given to those requesting information, free or low-cost access, and does not exceed the cost of copying and sending the information."[60]

The Council of Europe's Recommendation No. R(2002)2 on access to official documents contains significant detail on the standards which are applicable to requesting procedures, including:

- requests should be dealt with on an equal (non-discriminatory) basis and with a minimum of formality;
- applicants should not have to provide reasons for their requests;
- requests should be dealt with promptly and within established time limits;
- assistance should be provided "as far as possible"; and

[57] *See, e.g.*, National Security Archives, Eight Federal Agencies Have FOIA Requests a Decade Old, According to Knight Open Government Survey, July 4, 2011, http://nsarchive.gwu.edu/NSAEBB/NSAEBB349/.

[58] In an extreme case recently, a $660 million fee was assessed. *See* J. Pat Brown, *The Pentagon's $660 million FOIA fee: Secretary of Defense Estimates That Scouring Contract Data Would Take "15 Million Labor Hours,"* Feb. 26, 2016, https://www.muckrock.com/news/archives/2016/feb/26/biggest-foia-fee-all-time/.

[59] Joint Declaration, *supra* note 37.

[60] Principles on the Right of Access to Information, *supra* note 43.

- where they indicate a preference, applicants should be given access in that form, including inspection of the record or being given a copy.[61]

Despite having robust procedures in many respects, the U.S. act lost fourteen points over ten indicators in this category for these reasons:

1. The lack of a clear requirement for public authorities to have rules relating to the lodging of requests which are minimally onerous for requesters (Indicators 14 and 15, two points deducted, subparagraph (a)(3)(A)).
2. Limited obligations to provide assistance to requesters other than disabled persons (Indicator 16, two points deducted, clause (a)(3)(B)(ii) and subsection (l)).
3. Provision of a receipt acknowledging requests only where these take more than ten days to process (Indicator 18, one point deducted, paragraph (a)(7)).
4. The absence of any obligation to transfer requests where another public authority than the one which receives a request holds the information (Indicator 19, two points deducted).
5. The absence of any obligation to respond to requests as soon as possible, time limits of 20 working days (as opposed to the ideal of ten working days) and undue flexibility in terms of the length of extensions to the time limit (Indicators 21-23, four points deducted, paragraph (a)(6)).
6. The absence of limitations on fees to reproduction and sending the information or any obligation to waive fees for impecunious requesters (Indicators 25 and 26, three points deducted).

Looking at this category by age of the law does not yield the same conclusions as for scope. For example, the average score on this category for the ten latest laws was just 16.1 points, compared to 18.1 for the ten oldest, and it represented one of the weaker categories for the latest laws as compared to one of the stronger categories for the oldest laws. Interestingly, this category was also a relatively weaker area for the top ten laws (with an average score of just 22.2 points or 74%). Furthermore, no country managed to achieve an exceptional score in this category with Slovenia coming in top position here, albeit with just twenty-six out of a possible thirty points. The performance of the United States in this category was quite close to its overall average performance (53% vs. 55%) and this was also true for the full sample of countries (56% vs. 58%).

[61] Recommendation No. R (2012)2, Principles V-VII, *supra* note 42.

There may be various explanations for the relatively weaker performance of stronger and later laws, as compared to the median overall performance, in this category. The range and complexity of the indicators here may help explain the fact that even best practice counties lose a few points. It may also be that the extrapolated 'most enabling' approach resulted in more stringent standards here than for some other categories.

Exceptions and Refusals

The regime of exceptions is at the heart of an RTI law, as it defines the line between what shall be disclosed and what is secret. Theoretically, a law that did wonderfully in every other category could be almost entirely neutered by a weak regime of exceptions.[62] It is also the area where international standards are the most developed. This is due in part to the very extensive body of case law relating to restrictions on freedom of expression, which has established very clear rules and principles for this which are also applicable to the right to information.

Pursuant to Article 19(3) of the ICCPR, the right to freedom of expression is not absolute, and conditions for restrictions on the right are delineated:

> The exercise of the rights provided for in paragraph 2 of this article carries with it special duties and responsibilities. It may therefore be subject to certain restrictions, but these shall only be such as are provided by law and are necessary:
>
> (a) For respect of the rights or reputations of others;
> (b) For the protection of national security or of public order (ordre public), or of public health or morals.[63]

This imposes a strict and cumulative three-part test for the validity of any restriction on freedom of expression (cumulative in the sense that restrictions must pass all three parts of the test).[64] First, the restriction must be provided for by law. This requirement will be fulfilled only where the law is accessible and "formulated with sufficient precision to

[62]At its extreme, that is true of other categories, for example, because an otherwise perfect law that had no scope would not deliver any openness. But this problem seems to kick in much earlier for exceptions and is far more common in practice.

[63]International Covennt, on Civil and Political Rights, *supra* note 19.

[64]*See,* Mukong v. Cameroon, July 21, 1994, Communication No. 458/1991, paragraph 9.7 (UN Human Rights Committee).

enable the citizen to regulate his conduct."[65] In the context of the right to information, this rules out vague or unduly discretionary exceptions to the right of access.

Second, the restriction must be for the protection of a legitimate interest. The list of interests in Article 19(3) of the ICCPR is exclusive in the sense that these are the only interests the protection of which could justify a restriction on freedom of expression. Although this seems clear enough, in fact, it provides only limited guidance in the context of both the right to freedom of expression and the right to information. This is reflected, for example, in the very limited number of international cases which have been decided on the basis of this part of the test. In particular, the reference to the "rights" of others in Article 19(3)(a) has been interpreted very broadly by international courts, with the result that this part of the test has largely been deprived of any substance.

To resolve the fairly fundamental issue of which interests it accepts as being of sufficient importance to justify an exception to the right of access, the RTI Rating essentially combined this part of the test with the necessity part (discussed later), and a review of comparative practice. The underlying theory was that if a number of countries managed to do without an exception in favor of one or another particular interest, other countries could as well, and so protecting that interest through secrecy could not be justified as necessary.

In theory, the particular circumstances of a country could justify the protection of a unique or uncommon interest. In practice, however, the lack of real differences in terms of secrecy needs between countries, taking into account the relatively high level of generality at which the RTI Rating operates, meant that this theoretical construct was not actually relevant. That is not to suggest that the interpretation of exceptions could not vary, for example, based on local cultural values or the particular circumstances of a country. But the standards in the RTI Rating do not drill down to that level of detail. As noted previously, for example, the rating recognizes privacy as a legitimate interest which might justify secrecy, but it does not probe in any detail into what privacy means in practice, something which does vary among countries.[66] Similarly, countries' actual national security needs vary considerably based on a number of factors, but the principle that national security needs to

[65]The Sunday Times v. United Kingdom, Apr. 26, 1979, Application No. 6538/74, paragraph 49 (European Court of Human Rights).

[66]In practice, this is consistent with the approach taken in most RTI laws, which simply list privacy as a general value and leave its precise scope to future interpretation. In some cases, laws provide a list of privacy interests but these would be accepted by the rating unless there was some other flaw (for example, because they lacked a harm requirement).

be protected by secrecy, in appropriate cases (which would in practice need to be established by reference to actual facts), is established. This underlay the RTI Rating's recognition of national security as a legitimate interest to be protected by an exception.

The RTI Rating also recognizes that states may approach the specific protection of different legitimate interests in different ways. For example, one of the interests it recognizes as legitimate is the "prevention, investigation and prosecution of legal wrongs." There are numerous ways to do this and, as long as the approach taken remains within the scope of this interest, it is accepted by the Rating. Subsection (c) of the FOIA, for example, takes a rather unique approach to this issue, but no points were deducted on the United States rating assessment for this.

Third, according to Article 19(3) of the ICCPR, any restriction on freedom of expression must be necessary to protect the interest. The vast majority of international cases on freedom of expression are decided based on this part of the test, and, as a result, it usually attracts more attention and detailed analysis than the other parts. "Necessary" has been interpreted to encompass a number of elements, including that there must be a pressing social need for the restriction, that the means chosen to protect the interest is the least intrusive effective means available (that is, no less intrusive measure is available which would be effective), that the restriction is not overbroad in the sense that it only encompasses harmful speech, and that the restriction is not disproportionate in the sense that the harm caused by the restriction does not outweigh its benefits.[67]

In the context of the right to information, the necessity part of the test has a few implications beyond helping to define the interests which are considered to be worthy of protection *via* an exception. It means, first, that only information the disclosure of which would actually pose a risk of harm to a protected interest should be covered by an exception. It is fairly clear that, absent a risk of harm, the necessity of the exception cannot be made out. This leads to the idea that all exceptions should be harm tested (that is, include a reference to a risk of harm, as in "cause prejudice to national security" as opposed to simply relating to national security).

A second key implication of the necessity test is that all exceptions should be subject to what is often termed the public interest override, by which is meant a limit on the exception so that it applies only when

[67] *See, e.g.*, Lingens v. Austria, July 8, 1986, Application No. 9815/82, paragraphs 39-40 (European Court of Human Rights).

the benefits of secrecy (or protecting the interest) outweigh the harm done by secrecy (or are greater than the benefits that would accrue if the information were disclosed). This is a direct corollary of the proportionality part of the necessity test.

These standards are largely reflected in the Council of Europe Recommendation No. R(2002)2, which provides a detailed and exclusive list of the possible grounds for restricting the right to information in Principle IV, titled "Possible limitations to access to official documents":

> 1. Member states may limit the right of access to official documents. Limitations should be set down precisely in law, be necessary in a democratic society and be proportionate to the aim of protecting:
>   i. national security, defence and international relations;
>   ii. public safety;
>   iii. the prevention, investigation and prosecution of criminal activities;
>   iv. privacy and other legitimate private interests;
>   v. commercial and other economic interests, be they private or public;
>   vi. the equality of parties concerning court proceedings;
>   vii. nature;
>   viii. inspection, control and supervision by public authorities;
>   ix. the economic, monetary and exchange rate policies of the state;
>   x. the confidentiality of deliberations within or between public authorities during the internal preparation of a matter.
> 2. Access to a document may be refused if the disclosure of the information contained in the official document would or would be likely to harm any of the interests mentioned in paragraph 1, unless there is an overriding public interest in disclosure.[68]

Necessity also leads to some other standards in the RTI Rating, such as the idea of severability in Indicator 34. This calls for non-exempt information to be removed or redacted from a document and the rest of the document to be disclosed. Another standard which is derived from necessity, found in Indicator 32, is the idea of overall time limits, for example of fifteen or twenty years, for exceptions.

One of the more controversial standards in the rating, found in Indicator 28, is that the "standards in the RTI Law trump restrictions on information disclosure (secrecy provisions) in other legislation to the

[68]Recommendation No. R (2012)2, *supra* note 42.

extent of any conflict." Strictly speaking, it would be perfectly legitimate for a legal system to locate all of the exceptions to the right of access in other (secrecy) laws, as long as they in fact conformed to the standards noted above. In practice, however, in almost every country there are numerous secrecy provisions in other laws which fail to meet international standards, and the only practical way to address this in the short term is to provide for overriding effect for the RTI law.

The United States FOIA does not stipulate that it overrides conflicting legislation, although it does place some conditions on secrecy laws (paragraph (b)(3)), so earns one of four points under Indicator 28. Three exceptions in the act are not deemed to meet international standards, resulting in the loss of three points, namely the exception for internal personnel rules and practices (paragraph (b)(2)), because it is too broad, the exception for geological and geophysical information and data, including maps, concerning wells (paragraph (b)(9)), because it is not an interest that needs secrecy protection, and the foreign intelligence records exception (paragraph (c)(3)), because it is too broad and is also not harm tested. It should be noted, however, that this is actually a very respectable score on this Indicator, with most countries polling at or below this figure.

Three out of four points under Indicator 30 are lost for exceptions which do not include a harm test, including:

- information properly classified under an Executive order relating to national security or foreign policy (paragraph (b)(1));
- inter-agency or intra-agency memorandums or letters which would not be available by law to a party other than an agency in litigation with the agency (paragraph (b)(5)); and
- reports by agencies responsible for the regulation or supervision of financial institutions (paragraph (b)(8)).

The act also lacks a comprehensive public interest test.

The United States achieves an equal score in this category to the average score of the ten latest laws (57%), suggesting that this is not a particularly age sensitive category. On the other hand, seven of the ten latest law countries scored three or four points for harm testing exceptions, suggesting that this may be an area where performance has improved over time. Furthermore, the gap between the United States and the average of the top ten countries in this category (57% versus 78%) is almost exactly the same as the overall gap in averages (59% versus 83%). In other words, the comparative performance of the United States on this category is consistent with its overall average.

Appeals

It is in this area that the RTI Rating arguably diverges furthest from strict international legal standards. It is clear from general human rights principles that there should be a remedy where claims are made that human rights have been breached. Thus, Article 2(3) of the ICCPR states:

> Each State Party to the present Covenant undertakes:
>
> (a) To ensure that any person whose rights or freedoms as herein recognized are violated shall have an effective remedy, notwithstanding that the violation has been committed by persons acting in an official capacity;
> (b) To ensure that any person claiming such a remedy shall have his right thereto determined by competent judicial, administrative or legislative authorities, or by any other competent authority provided for by the legal system of the State, and to develop the possibilities of judicial remedy; and
> (c) To ensure that the competent authorities shall enforce such remedies when granted.[69]

But, as even the language of this provision suggests, international law does not prescribe the precise nature of the remedy that should be made available.

As regards the right to information, it is clear that requesters need to be able to avail themselves of an appeal to an independent body where they are refused access to information by a public authority. Otherwise, the right of access essentially lies at the discretion of the public authority, and hence cannot be described as a right. That public authorities have strong vested interests in the release or otherwise of information further highlights this need.

The idea of an appeal is firmly reflected in soft law standards relating to the right to information. Thus, Council of Europe Recommendation No. R(2002)2 refers to the right to appeal to a "court of law or another independent and impartial body established by law."[70] The Declaration of Principles on Freedom of Expression in Africa, for its part, refers to two levels of appeal, "to an independent body and/or the courts."[71] The Inter-American Juridical Committee's Principles on the Right of Access

[69] International Covenant on Civil and Political Rights, *supra* note 19.
[70] Recommendation No. R (2012)2, *supra* note 42, at Principle IX(1).
[71] Declaration of Principles on Freedom of Expression in Africa, *supra* note 41, at Principle IV(2).

to Information also call for two levels of appeal, to "an administrative jurisdiction" and to the courts.[72]

Despite the somewhat equivocal nature of these statements, the experience of countries around the world has been that the presence of an independent administrative level of appeal provides a huge boost to efforts to implement RTI laws effectively.[73] This is, in part, because appeals to the courts, which are the other main option, are simply too costly and time consuming to be accessible or practical for the vast majority of requesters. But it is also in part due to the wider role many administrative appellate bodies play in terms of providing positive support for implementation efforts.

For these reasons, the RTI Rating focuses quite heavily in this category on the existence and qualities of administrative oversight bodies, alongside a number of other positive appeal features, such as having broad grounds for appeals, and placing the burden on public authorities to justify refusals to provide access.

The United States does not provide for an administrative level of appeal relating to the right to information, and so necessarily loses all of the points for Indicators 38-43,[74] resulting in a poor overall score in this category, despite doing well on most of the other indicators here.

It is tempting to attribute the lack of an administrative oversight system in the United States to the early adoption of the law, and amendments in 2007 did very partially address this problem by at least creating the Office of Government Information Services (paragraph (h)(1)), which has the power to offer mediation services to resolve disputes between requesters and public authorities (paragraph (h)(3)). However, Sweden had an ombudsman based oversight system as early as 1810,[75] and of the nine other ten earliest laws (that is, other than the United States), fully eight provide for an administrative oversight body. Indeed, this is one of the few categories where the oldest laws outperform the latest laws, by a margin of 64% to 55%.

---

[72]Principles on the Right of Access to Information, *supra* note 43, at Principle 8.

[73]*See, e.g.,* OAS Special Rapporteur for Freedom of Expression, The Right to Access to Public Information in the Americas: Specialized Supervisory and Enforcement Bodies, March 2015, *available at* http://www.oas.org/en/iachr/expression/docs/reports/ACCESS/Thematic%20Report%20access%20To%20public%20information%20 2014.pdf; LAURA NEUMAN, ENFORCEMENT MODELS: CONTENT AND CONTEXT (2009), *available at* http://siteresources.worldbank.org/EXTGOVACC/Resources/LNEumanATI.pdf.

[74]These indicators look at the presence and various attributes of an administrative oversight body.

[75]The first ombudsman, Lars August Mannerheim, was formally appointed in 1810 with responsibilities that included overview of the right to information system. Information provided by Swedish lawyer Per Hultengård, on file with the author.

Sanctions and Protections, and Promotional Measures

The rules in the RTI Rating on sanctions and protections are, once again, largely derived from soft law statements, as well as the practical experience of different countries in these areas. The 2004 Joint Declaration of the special international mandates on freedom of expression calls for "sanctions for those who wilfully obstruct access to information,"[76] while the Declaration of Principles on Freedom of Expression in Africa states: "[N]o one shall be subject to any sanction for releasing in good faith information on wrongdoing, or that which would disclose a serious threat to health, safety or the environment save where the imposition of sanctions serves a legitimate interest and is necessary in a democratic society."[77]

The RTI Rating calls for two types of sanctions – for willful obstruction of access by individuals and for systemic failures by public authorities to meet their openness obligations – and two types of protections – for individuals who release information pursuant to the law in good faith and for individuals who release information about wrongdoing (whistleblowers).

In the United States, there are laws preventing the destruction of documents[78] and disciplinary actions can be undertaken under the act in limited circumstances,[79] but there are no general rules on sanctions for willful obstruction of access. Similarly, there are only limited systems for imposing measures on public authorities which structurally fail to respect the act. The United States has strong rules on whistleblower protection[80] but it fails to provide formal legal protection to those who release information pursuant to the FOIA. The latter is important, among other things, to give individuals the confidence to release such information.

Promotional measures is another category of the RTI Rating where standards are extrapolated largely from a 'most enabling' approach towards discharging positive obligations, better comparative practice and soft law statements. This is the category where the FOIA does by far the best, fully 15 percentage points ahead of any other category, with twelve out of sixteen points, or 75%. This is based on strong provisions relating to issues such as the appointment of specialized officials to deal with requests (the Chief FOIA Officers, subsections (j) and

[76]Joint Declaration, *supra* note 37.

[77]Declaration of Principles of Freedom of Expression in Africa, *supra* note 41, at Principle IV(2).

[78]*See* Records Management by Federal Agencies, 44 U.S.C. §3106 (1968).

[79]*Id.* at (a)(4)(F)(i).

[80]*Id.* at § 1201 (Prohibited Personnel Practices).

(k)), the existence of a lead body for undertaking promotional measures (the Office of Government Information Services, subsection (h)), and very detailed reporting requirements for both public authorities and the Attorney General (subsection (e)). Two points are lost in this category due to the lack of any obligation on public authorities to publish lists of the records that they hold, and another two are lost due to the failure to impose any formal obligation on public bodies to train their officials (although it is recognized that in practice training is widely provided in the United States).

Conclusions

As the third country in the world to adopt a law giving individuals a right to access information held by public bodies, or the right to information, the United States was, by definition, a global leader in this area. As it celebrates the fiftieth anniversary of the adoption of this groundbreaking legislation, the United States can look back proudly on the leading role it has played globally in terms of putting in place RTI legislation.

In terms of the quality of the FOIA, however, according to the RTI Rating, the leading global methodology for assessing the legal framework for the right to information, the United States sits at an unremarkable fifty-first position globally out of 103 countries. Given the fact that the FOIA has been regularly amended and improved, and that the RTI Rating is based on a set of minimum human rights standards, this is a cause for some concern. Particular areas of weakness are protection for the right of access, the system for lodging appeals against refusals to provide information, and the set of sanctions and protections for obstructing or disclosing information, all of which score 50% or lower on the RTI Rating.

In some cases, the weaknesses of the FOIA find resonance among other older RTI laws, with many of the other older laws suffering from the same flaws. Thus, few early adopters included the legislative and judicial branches of government within the scope of their RTI laws. However, in the United States, unlike in some other early adopting countries, the RTI law has been amended on a number of occasions. While these successive amendments have contributed to somewhat improved scores on the RTI Rating, they have done little to address the main structural flaws, raising questions as to why this might be.

In other cases, the FOIA's shortcomings do not appear to be based on the era in which it was adopted. The absence of an administrative body which has the power to decide on appeals regarding the way requests for information were processed, for example, is an area where, in general, the early adopters actually do better than the later adopters. The United States does not seem to be able to move forward strongly on this issue, despite having established a central support body with the power to mediate disputes, in the form of the Office of Government Information Services.

Anecdotal evidence, along with some high profile instances of whistle-blowing, notably the Edward Snowden disclosures, suggests that in practice the United States remains among the more open countries globally. Efforts to amend the legal framework for RTI so as to reflect better international standards in this area could only further bolster openness in practice.

THE NEWS MEDIA AND THE FOIA

DERIGAN SILVER

Journalists were at the forefront of the effort to pass the Freedom of Information Act. News organizations were intrinsically involved in crafting the legislation and were a key factor in making sure the law was passed. For many reasons, however, FOIA has frequently failed to meet the news media's needs. One reason the law is failing is because journalists do not use it nearly as much as non-media requesters, a fact that stands in stark contrast to the history and purpose of the law. The purpose of this article is to explore data on who uses FOIA. In addition, it examines reasons journalists are not using the law, offers some practical reforms that could improve FOIA, and suggests advice on how journalists could better craft their FOIA requests. It also concludes, however, that despite its flaws, journalists are still using FOIA to write stories that advance self-government and the watchdog function of the press, and there is reason to believe a new generation of journalists are using FOIA in new and inventive ways.

Journalists were at the forefront of the effort to pass the Freedom of Information Act. [1] The Supreme Court of the United States noted the law was intended to protect the public's right to know[2] and to help serve as a check on government.[3] Not only was the law intended to be used by journalists, journalists were intrinsically involved in crafting the legislation.[4] As Professors Shannon E. Martin and Kamilla Benko noted, while Congressmen John Moss and others deserve much of the credit for passing FOIA, Moss and his staff "relied heavily on the expertise

[1] 5 U.S.C. § 552 (2012).

[2] U.S. Dep't of Justice v. Reporters Comm. for Freedom of the Press, 489 U.S. 749, 773 (1989).

[3] NLRB v. Robbins Tire & Rubber Co., 437 U.S. 214, 242 (1978) (Marshall, J., dissenting).

[4] *See infra* notes 15-49 and accompanying text.

of long-time activists who fought for access to government documents"[5] including the American Society of Newspaper Editors, the Society of Professional Journalists, and the Associated Press Managing Editors. A review of the legislative history of the act, makes it clear that the law was intended to help the media inform the public about government operations and thus advance democratic participation in government[6] and facilitate the press's ability to act as a check on government abuse,[7] two of the most fundamental theories concerning the role of freedom of expression and the press in a democratic society.[8] As the 1964 House of Representatives Report on access laws declared, "A democratic society requires an informed, intelligent electorate and the intelligence of the electorate varies as the quantity and quality of its information."[9] In addition, journalists believe access laws are important tools, with one study showing that 97% of journalists believe open records laws are important for them to fulfill their duties.[10]

It is ironic then, that while FOIA has been criticized for a variety of reasons,[11] its most notable disappointment has been its "failure to meet the news media's information needs."[12] While FOIA is failing journalists for many reasons — most notably, as discussed below, the long delays and processing inefficiencies associated with access requests — a key reason the law is failing journalists is because journalists simply do not use it nearly as much as corporations and other non-media

[5]Sharon E. Martin & Kamilla Benko, *Forming FOIA: The Influence of Editors and Publishers on the Freedom of Information Act*, 14 Media Hist. Monographs 1, 2 (2011).

[6]*See generally* Alexander Meiklejohn, Free Speech and Its Relation to Self-Government (1948) (discussing of freedom of expression as a necessary right so that the electorate may be informed enough to participate in self-government).

[7]*See generally* Vincent Blasi, *The Checking Value in First Amendment Theory*, 3 Am. B. Found. Res. J. 521 (1977) (discussing of the need for freedom of expression so that the press may serve as a check on government).

[8]*See* Heidi Kitrosser, *Secrecy in the Immigration Courts and Beyond: Considering the Right to Know in the Administrative State*, 39 Harv. C.R.-C.L. L. Rev. 95, 126-30 (2004) (discussing the self-government and watchdog functions of freedom of expression as they relate to freedom of information laws).

[9]S. Rep. No. 88-1219, at 8 (1964).

[10]*See* Charles Davis, *Stacked Deck Favors Government Secrecy*, IRE J., Mar./Apr. 2002, at 14.

[11]*See, e.g.*, Margaret B. Kwoka, *Deferring to Secrecy*, 54 B.C. L. Rev. 185 (2013) (providing ample evidence that courts give overwhelming deference to administrative agencies' decisions to not release information); Antonin Scalia, *The Freedom of Information Act Has No Clothes*, Reg. Mar./Apr. 1982, at 14, 15 (discussing the inefficiency of FOIA and the law's poor cost-benefit ratio); Statement of Adina Rosenbaum, Staff Attorney, Public Citizen, before the Information Policy, Census, and National Archives Subcommittee, Oversight and Government Reform Committee, United States House of Representatives (Mar. 18, 2010) (documenting the over-withholding of information under FOIA).

[12]Margaret B. Kwoka, *FOIA, Inc.*, 65 Duke L. J. 1361, 1364 (2016).

individuals and organizations, a fact that stands in stark contrast to the history and purpose of the law.

The purpose of this article is to explore data on who uses FOIA. Although a comprehensive study of FOIA use in every agency governed by the legislation has never been conducted — and conducting such a study would be extremely difficult[13] — several studies have looked at specific federal agencies to examine who makes requests. The article begins by reviewing the legislative history of FOIA and scholarship that has examined the role of news media organizations in crafting and passing the legislation. It then contrasts the clear purpose of the legislation with the equally clear reality that the law is not being used as intended by analyzing data about FOIA requests. The article concludes that while the exact number of requests made by media organizations is difficult to calculate, it is clear that such requests have historically represented an extremely small minority of overall requests. Finally, the article explores some possible explanations for why journalists represent such a small minority of requesters and offers practical suggestions for both how journalists can improve their FOIA requests and how the government could facilitate access by journalists.

The article also suggests that, even if media requests do not make up the majority of FOIA requests, this is not an appropriate metric for addressing the question, "Do journalists use FOIA *enough*?" The public's interest in accessing government information remains high. During the last two fiscal years, more than 700,000 FOIA requests were received by federal agencies.[14] The article suggests it is acceptable that journalists are not the primary users of FOIA even if the law was originally intended to be used primarily by journalists. While there are legitimate concerns that the large number of these requests that do not relate to the ability of the press to monitor and report on the government slow down the process and impede journalists from successfully obtaining information via FOIA, the article argues that some journalists are using the law quite successfully to gather information to help the press inform the public and act as a watchdog over government. The article concludes there is reason to believe a new generation of journalists may be using FOIA in new and inventive ways.

[13]See *infra* notes 50-54 and accompanying text. As discussed below, while agencies keep FOIA logs of the FOIA requests they receive, not all of these logs record the identity of a requester.

[14]Department of Justice, Summary of Annual FOIA Reports for Fiscal Year 2014, 2 (2016), https://www.justice.gov/sites/default/files/oip/pages/attachments/2015/05/01/fy_2014_annual_report_summary.pdf.

THE HISTORY AND PURPOSE OF FOIA

Although scholars have argued that access to government information is a constitutional right[15] and at least two international courts have declared access to government information a human right,[16] in the United States and much of the world, access to government information is guaranteed by statutory law.[17] While government transparency has taken hold across the globe,[18] the United States was a leader in the modern movement to pass access laws. When the United States enacted FOIA in 1966, it was the second country to enact a freedom of information law.[19] As in most cases with freedom of information laws, FOIA was brought about by concentrated political activism. As Professor Mark Fenster noted, "Government transparency does not spring naturally from the modern democratic state."[20] In the case of FOIA, much of the lobbying for the law came directly from news media and journalism organizations. Professor Kiyyul Uhm wrote that the right to know movement cannot be classified as a public movement, because the general public did not actively participate.[21] Professor Fenster found the freedom to information movement to be driven by political economy of the international news industry, the Associated Press's struggle with European news cartels, a post-World War II emergent ideal of press freedom, and the American press' conception of journalism as "a vocation organized around the objective reporting of news."[22] Against this backdrop, the phrases "freedom of information" and "the right to know" were purposely advanced by members of the press.

---

[15]*See, e.g.*, Thomas I. Emerson, *The Amendment and the Right to Know: Legal Foundations of the Right to Know*, 1976 WASH. U. L.Q. 1 (1976).

[16]In 2006, the Inter-American Court of Human Rights declared access to government information to be included within the human rights of free thought and freedom of expression. *See* Reyes v. Chile, Inter-Am. Ct. H.R. (ser. C) No. 151, ¶ 77 (Sept. 19, 2006). In 2009, the European Court of Human rights did the same. *See* Társaság a Szabadságjogokért v. Hungary, App. No. 37374/05, ¶ 39 (Apr. 14, 2009).

[17]In the United States, the notable exception to this is access to court documents, which is secured *via* the First Amendment. *See* Press-Enterprise Co. v. Superior Court, 478 U.S. 1, 13 (1986) (finding the First Amendment right of access to criminal trials also extends to judicial documents).

[18]*Chronological and Alphabetical List of Countries with FOI Regimes*, FREEDOMOFINFO.ORG, http://www.freedominfo.org/2016/04/chronological-and-alphabetical-lists-of-countries-with-foi-regimes/.

[19]*Id.* Sweden was far in front of even the United States, enacting its freedom to information law in 1766.

[20]Mark Fenster, *The Transparency Fix: Advocating Legal Rights and Their Alternatives in the Pursuit of a Visible State*, 73 U. PITT. L. REV. 443, 446 (2012).

[21]Kiyul Uhm, *The Cold War Communication Crisis: The Right to Know Movement*, 82 JOURNALISM & MASS COMM. Q. 131, 132 (2005).

[22]Fenster, *supra* note 20, at 458.

The push to enact a federal freedom of information statute began in earnest in the 1940s, although the movement has its roots in the decades following World War I as newspaper editors and journalism associations "actively worked to export abroad the American model of a private, for-profit press insulated from government oversight and censorship."[23] The roots of the movement came from the twin desires of opening foreign markets to American media corporations and exporting the American ideal of a free press.[24] A cartel of major European new agencies, including Reuters, Agence Havas, and Wolff, divided the world into geographic territories for newsgathering, and members of the cartel agreed to only publish information from other cartel members.[25] While the AP joined the cartel in 1887, it began to feel constrained by its membership when domestic news consumption increased. Competition from United Press, which was not restrained by membership in the cartel, also increased, and the AP started gathering news internationally.[26] Historian Margaret Blanchard noted the AP was also highly concerned with the European news agencies' close ties to national governments that shaped news content.[27] In response to concerns over the control of international news gathering and distribution, European news media's close ties to national governments, and the lack of objective news values that came from foreign news agencies, the AP launched an international effort to promote press freedom and access to government information and create independent news media around the globe to compete with the cartel.[28] After emerging commercially victorious, the American media "turned evangelical"[29] about press freedom and the need for access to government information.

In 1944, the American Society of Newspaper Editors announced a campaign to advocate for freedom of information around the world.[30] This included a collaboration with the Harry Truman administration to spur development of international news organizations that would be based on the American model of an independent press with professional trained journalists.[31] In 1947, members of the press played roles on the UN's Human Rights commission sub-commission on Free-

[23] *Id.* at 451.
[24] *Id.*
[25] *Id.* at 451-52.
[26] *Id.* at 452.
[27] Margaret Blanchard, Exporting the First Amendment 6-7 (1986).
[28] *See* Fenster, *supra* note 20, at 453.
[29] *Id.*
[30] *See id.*
[31] *See* Blanchard, *supra* note 27, at 52-89.

dom of Information[32] and served as delegates to the Conference on Freedom of Information held in Geneva in 1948.[33] There were also efforts to promote press freedom and access to information at home. In 1944, the ASNE formed the Committee on World Freedom of Information to advance international goals related to access to information.[34] In 1945, Kent Cooper, the powerful and influential general manager of the AP, authored an article for *Life* magazine titled "Freedom of Information."[35] In 1956, Cooper followed up his article with a book on access to information, which he titled *The Right to Know*, and argued both for the freedom to gather news and that the press was ethically bound to give the public information in order to promote self-government.[36]

The two most prominent proponents of the right to know movement were James S. Pope, editor of the *Louisville Courier-Journal,* and Harold L. Cross, legal advisor to the ASNE's Freedom of Information Committee.[37] Pope recruited Cross to write *The People's Right to Know*,[38] which was published in 1953. The book both detailed the current state of constitutional and administrative laws governing access to information and government secrecy at the federal, state, and municipal levels[39] and advocated for additional freedom of information laws at the federal level.[40]

Shortly after Cross's book was published, the right to know movement found an ally in Congress when the House of Representatives Government Operations Committee established a Special Subcommittee on Government Information, chaired by California Representative John Moss, as a means to investigate Executive Branch secrecy.[41] The

[32]*See id.* at 155-63.

[33]*Id.* at 174-97.

[34]*See* Uhm, *supra* note 21, at 139. While Professor Uhm noted the term "free flow of information" was a more popular term than "right to know" in the 1940s and 1950s, the term "freedom of information" was in use throughout the 1940s. President Franklin Delano Roosevelt used it as early as 1940 to refer to the free flow of news. *See* CASS SUNSTEIN, THE SECOND BILL OF RIGHTS: FDR'S UNFINISHED REVOLUTION AND WHY WE NEED IT MORE THAN EVER 78-79 (2004).

[35]Kent Cooper, *Freedom of Information: Head of Associated Press Calls for Unhampered Flow of World News*, LIFE, Nov. 13, 1944, at 55.

[36]KENT COOPER, THE RIGHT TO KNOW: AN EXPOSITION OF THE EVILS OF NEWS SUPPRESSION AND PROPAGANDA (1956).

[37]*See* Uhm, *supra* note 21, at 134.

[38]HAROLD CROSS, THE PEOPLE'S RIGHT TO KNOW (1953).

[39]*Id.* at 19-37.

[40]*Id.* at 246 (calling on Congress to "legislate freedom of information for itself, the public, and the press").

[41]*See* MICHAEL R. LEMOV, PEOPLE'S WARRIOR: JOHN MOSS AND THE FIGHT FOR FREEDOM OF INFORMATION AND CONSUMER RIGHTS 49 (2011).

ASNE Freedom of Information Committee was quick to begin working with the subcommittee, with Cross becoming its legal advisor, former journalists making up most of its staff, and prominent members of the media helping to devise its strategy.[42] Pope testified at the subcommittee's first hearing, again using the rhetoric that access to government information was not a political issue, but a legal right.[43] The so-called "Moss Committee" routinely called journalists to testify to both document the difficulties in gaining access to government information and to gain publicity for the committee's work.[44] Based on the work of Moss, Cross and Pope, the Freedom of Information Act – whose very name was taken from a journalists 1949 book[45] — finally passed Congress in 1966.

Thus, FOIA was largely designed by journalists. On the floor when FOIA was passed, Moss stated, "The list of editors, broadcasters and newsmen and distinguished members for the corps who have helped develop the legislation over these 10 years is endless."[46] In addition, FOIA's history supports the concept that its intended purpose was for journalists to use the law to facilitate democratic self-government and act as a government watchdog. Professor Margaret Kwoka noted, "FOIA was . . . designed largely by journalists, for journalists, and with the particular goal in mind that journalists would use access to government information to provide knowledge to the public, which would, in turn, facilitate the public's effective participation in democratic governance."[47] Professor Fenster wrote that the press worked with the state to create the law under the assumption that "the press, acting as the public's agent, would advance and take advantage of the right to know."[48] Professor Kwoka also noted that of the 176 complaints about government secrecy collected by the Moss committee, "37 percent were from journalists and 45 percent from Congress itself, suggesting an outsized role for journalists in using any new freedom of information law."[49] The data, however, suggest that journalists are not the primary requesters of information under the law.

[42] *See* Fenster, *supra* note 20, at 464.
[43] *See* Uhm, *supra* note 21, at 140.
[44] *See* Robert O. Blanchard, *Present at the Creation: The Media and the Moss Committee*, 49 JOURNALISM Q. 271, 272-74 (1972).
[45] *See id.* at 276.
[46] 112 CONG. REC. 13,642-43 (1966).
[47] Kwoka, *supra* note 12, at 1371.
[48] Fenster, *supra* note 20, at 466.
[49] *Id.*

FOIA Requests by Journalists

As one scholar wrote, "Very little is known about who uses the FOIA or how it is used."[50] There has never been a comprehensive study of who makes FOIA requests across the federal government.[51] Definitively answering what percent of FOIA requests are filed by journalists or news organizations is difficult because not all agencies report the identity of requesters. Agencies keep FOIA logs or lists of requests for information received that contain information about the requests. In addition, many agencies post their FOIA logs online.[52] If a log is not available online, one may obtain it by using a Freedom of Information Request, a process sometimes described as "FOIA the FOIAs." The information in the logs sometimes, but not always, includes a description of the information being requested, the name and/or organization making the request, the date the request was received, and the current status or final outcome of the requests (for example, granted, denied, partially granted). However, not all FOIA logs contain all of this information. For example, the Securities and Exchange Commission FOIA log contains the request identification, the requester's name and organization, requester category, request description, request date, and final outcome.[53] On the other hand, the FOIA logs for the U.S. State Department contain only the requester's name, making it difficult to determine if the requester is a member of the media.[54]

Another possible tool for researching media use of FOIA is by examining fees. The FOIA fee structure, added in a 1986 amendment, allows for different categories of users to be charged different fees. There are four categories: commercial, media, nonprofit (scientific and edu-

[50]Raymond M. Lee, *Research Uses of the U.S. Freedom of Information Act*, 13 Field Methods 370, 370 (2001).

[51]*See* Kwoka, *supra* note 12, at 1376.

[52]*See, e.g.*, U.S. Department of Homeland Security Component FOIA Logs, https://www.dhs.gov/dhs-component-foia-logs (last visited Jun. 28, 2016)(Web site containing links to the last three years of FOIA logs for U.S. Customs and Boarder Protection, Office of Civil Rights and Civil Liberties, Federal Emergency Management Agency, Federal Law Enforcement Training Center, Office of Intelligence and Analysis, U.S Immigration and Customs Enforcement, Management Directorate, National Protection and Programs Directorate, Office of Biometric Identity Management, Office of General Counsel, Office of Operations Coordination, office of Policy, Science and Technology Directorate, Transportation and Security Administration, United States Citizenship and Immigration Services, United States Coast Guard, and United States Secret Service.)

[53]*See, e.g.*, U.S. Security and Exchange Commission FOIA Logs, https://www.sec.gov/foia/docs/foia-logs.htm (last visited Jun. 28, 2016).

[54]*See, e.g.*, U.S. State Department FOIA Logs (2005-2013), https://foia.state.gov/Search/Logs.aspx#2014 (last visited Jun. 28, 2016).

cational) and other. For commercial requests, agencies, can charge fees for "reasonable standard charges for document search, duplication, and review."[55] Only duplication charges are made for a request by "an educational or noncommercial scientific institution, whose purpose is scholarly or scientific research; or a representative of the news media."[56] Under FOIA, a representative of the news media is "any person or entity that gathers information of potential interest to a segment of the public, uses its editorial skills to turn the raw materials into a distinct work, and distributes that work to an audience."[57] FOIA defines "news" as "information that is about current events or that would be of interest to the public."[58] Unfortunately, most FOIA logs do not classify requests by fee status.[59] In addition, if a freelance journalist or citizen journalist were to file a FOIA request and not list an organization with the request or not specifically ask for the non-commercial fee, there would be virtually no way to know the request was a media request. There are additional problems. If an agency has a complete log, and the log is the subject of a FOIA request, a response is often long in coming.[60] Or, the agency may redact the identity of the requester citing privacy concerns or other FOIA exemptions,[61] or not respond at all.[62] In addition, agencies may keep incomplete logs that do not include useful information about requesters.[63] Agencies also frequently designate non-media entities as news media[64] or inconsistently categorize an organization.[65] Therefore, although agencies provide information about the FOIA requests they receive, there are multiple roadblocks to conducting a complete survey of FOIA requests by the media.

All agencies governed by FOIA also are required to file annual reports. While it would be easy for agencies to include information

---

[55] 5 U.S.C. § 552(a)(4)(A)(ii)(I) (2012).

[56] *Id.* § 552(a)(4)(A)(ii)(II).

[57] *Id.*

[58] *Id.*

[59] *See* Lee, *supra* note 50, at 373.

[60] *Frequent Filers: Businesses make FOIA Their Business*, SOCIETY OF PROFESSIONAL JOURNALISTS, Jul. 3, 2006, http://www.spj.org/rrr.asp?ref=31&t=foia)(noting that 25% of 199 departments who received FOIA requests for their FOIA logs did not respond within the required twenty working days)[hereinafter Frequent Filers].

[61] *Id.*

[62] *Id.*

[63] *See* Kwoka, *supra* note 12, at 1380 (discussing the difficulties of getting complete FOIA logs from agencies). Professor Kwoka described a "complete" log as one that contained a request tracking number, the date of the request, the identity of the requester, the subject matter of the request, the requester's fee category, the actual fee charged to the requester, and the agency's response. *Id.* at 1380-81.

[64] *See id.* at 1384, 1388.

[65] *Id.* at 1390.

about fee status in these reports, most agencies do not.[66] When an agency reports this information, it is easy to determine the percentage of requests that come from media organizations. For example, in 1998 and 1999, the Environmental Protection Agency provided information about requesters' fee status in its annual reports. In 1998, 1% of requests were from media organizations, while in 1999 1.2% of requests were from media organizations.[67] Unfortunately, since at least 2007, the EPA no longer includes this data in its annual reports.[68] In addition, the EPA currently groups media requesters together with educational requesters in its FOIA logs and it is unclear if they did this in their 1998 and 1999 reports as well.

Despite these obstacles to a complete study of FOIA requests, a number of studies of samples of requests that are based on FOIA logs with information about requesters' categories or identities. Professor Raymond M. Lee analyzed five years of data from the Federal Bureau of Investigation. In 1995, requests from news media made up 3.3% of all FOIA requests to the FBI.[69] In 1996, the number dropped to 2.6% percent and continued to drop in 1997 when it hit a bottom of 1.6 percent.[70] Starting in 1998, the number of requests by news media organizations began to increase and continued to increase until 2000. In 1998, 2.3% of requests were made by media organizations, increasing to 4.8 percent in 1999 and 6.5% in 2000.[71] It should be noted that Professor Lee did not explain how he classified the identity of requesters to determine when a request should be attributed to a member of the news media. Current FBI FOIA logs only contain a requester's name, which may or may not include an organization and do not contain fee categories.[72]

A 2005 review of five years of FOIA logs from the Pentagon concluded journalists from large media organizations made a very small number of requests.[73] Of the more than 10,000 requests received by the Pentagon from 2000 to 2005, the Associated Press made seventy-three

[66] *See* Lee, *supra* note 50, at 373.

[67] *See id.*

[68] *See* ENVIRONMENTAL PROTECTION AGENCY FOI REPORTS, https://www.epa.gov/foia/foia-reports#annual (last visited Jun2 28, 2016). Like most agencies, the EPA now only reports the total amount of revenue generated by fees.

[69] Lee, *supra* note 50, at 374.

[70] *Id.*

[71] *Id.*

[72] *See, e.g.*, FEDERAL BUREAU OF INVESTIGATION FREEDOM OF INFORMATION ACT LOG 1/1/2013 TO 3/31/2013, https://d3gn0r3afghep.cloudfront.net/foia_files/FOIA_LOG_1-1-2013_TO_3-31-2013.PDF (last visited June 28, 2016).

[73] John Byrne, *Freedom of Information Logs She Light on Media's Military Curiosity*, THE RAW STORY, Nov. 23, 2005, http://rawstory.com/news/2005/Freedom_of_Information_logs_shed_light_1123.html.

requests, the *Los Angeles Times* made forty-two, the *Washington Post* made thirty-four, the *New York Times* made twenty-one, *USA Today* made nine, and the *Wall Street Journal* made six.[74] CBS News made thirty-two requests, Fox News made twenty-two requests, NBC News made twenty-one requests, and CNN made eleven.[75]

In 2006, the Coalition of Journalists for Open Government analyzed 6,439 FOIA requests made in September 2005 to eleven Cabinet-level departments and six agencies.[76] The review found that requests from media organizations made up only 6% percent of all requests. The coalition requested FOIA logs from twelve departments and eight agencies, but did not include the three agencies that receive the most requests — the Department of Veterans Affairs, the Department of Health and Human Services, and the Social Security Administration — because more than 90% of requests to these agencies are also filed under the Privacy Act and are filed by individuals seeking personal information.[77] The coalition relied upon the logs to classify a requester as a media requester when the logs indicated a fee category for a requester.[78] The coalition made its own determination when no category was provided, although there is no explanation in the report of how these determinations were made.[79] While the study found that the top requester to each agency varied greatly by agency because of "special-interest" users,[80] no agency reported a majority of requests coming from media organizations.

The most recent analysis of FOIA logs was conducted by Professor Kwoka and focused on commercial users of FOIA and used data from fiscal year 2013.[81] Although Professor Kwoka made FOIA requests for FOIA logs from twenty-three federal agencies,[82] she was only able to get complete FOIA logs that included the fee category of the requester from the Securities and Exchange Commission, Food and Drug Admin-

[74]*Id.*

[75]*Id.*

[76]*Frequent Filers, supra* note 60.

[77]*Id.*

[78]*Id.*

[79]*Id.*

[80]For example, nearly all requests to the Parole Commission came from prisoners while the Defense Supply Center received "99 percent of their requests from companies seeking records on government contracts." *Id.*

[81]Kwoka, *supra* note 12.

[82]Professor Kwoka's research examined the use of FOIA by commercial requesters. Therefore, she only sent FOIA request to agencies that received more than one thousand requests in fiscal year 2013 and collected more than $10,000 in free from requesters. Because commercial requesters are most often charged fees and charged the largest fees this procedure targeted agencies with high levels of commercial requesting. *Id.* at 1379.

istration, Environmental Protection Agency, Defense Logistics Agency, Federal Trade Commission, and the National Institutes of Health.

The only agency that reported a significant portion of media requests was the FTC. News media requests constituted 14% of the FTC's requests in 2013. In every other agency, however, FOIA requests from news media were even lower than the 6% reported by the Coalition of Journalists for Open Government. Five percent of requests to the NIH were made by news media.[83] Less than 1% of requests to the DLA were classified as media requesters.[84] As noted above, the EPA groups news media and educational requesters together, making it difficult to know exactly how many requests came from the media. However, at least 1.8% of requesters were definitely news media or quasi-media.[85]

According to the FDA's classification of fees, news media filed 12% of the requests to the agency.[86] However, many of the organizations classified as news media by the FDA were information resellers. Traditional news media organizations only accounted for 2% of the requests.[87] Similarly, at first glance, the SEC FOIA logs indicated that a much higher percentage of requests come from journalists than suggested by the 2006 coalition study. The SEC classified news media requests as 23% of the total it received in FY 2003.[88] However, this number is deceptive. Of the 2,807 requests the SEC classified as news media, 2,498 came from SECProbes.com.[89] As Professor Kwoka details in her research, SECProbes.com is a non-functioning Web site registered to a John Gavin, a "former money manager,"[90] who founded a company called SEC Insight that specialized in selling information obtained *via*

[83]*Id.* at 1410.

[84]*Id.* at 1401.

[85]*Id.* Media organizations or quasi-media organizations making at least five requests were MuckRock News, EnergyWire/E&E Publishing, Environmental Integrity Project, The Center for Investigative Reporting, the Associated Press, Reuters, the *Washington Examiner*, *The Hill*, the *Huffington Post*, ProPublica, Junksceince.com, and the *Wall Street Journal*.

[86]*Id.* at 1388

[87]*Id.* at 1397. The FDA either inconsistently categorized commercial requesters or classified information resellers as media organizations. Media organizations or quasi-media organizations making at least five requests were the *Wall Street Journal*, Bloomberg News, The Project on Government Oversight, *USA Today*, ProPublica, the Associated Press, the *New York Times*, WSB-TV in Atlanta, Scripps Howard News Service, CNN, MSNBC.com, and the Natural Resources Defense Council. *Id.*

[88]*Id.* at 1382.

[89]*Id.*

[90]*See* Gretchen Morgenson, *Deafened by the S.E.C.'s Silence, He Sued*, N.Y. TIMES, May 28, 2006, *available at* http://www.nytimes.com/2006/05/28/business/yourmoney/28gavin.html?_r=0.

FOIA requests to mutual funds and hedge funds.[91] SEC Insight was categorized as a commercial requester and went out of business in 2012.[92] SECProbes, now classified as a news media requester, appears to be making requests on behalf of a new company founded by Gavin called "Probes Reporter," which has a similar business model to SEC Insight.[93] In addition, a law firm's thirty-seven requests were also classified as news media requests.[94] Without SECProbes.com's and the law firm's requests, only 2.2% of the requests came from news media.

There is also evidence media organizations are litigating FOIA denials at a lower rate. A 2009 study by the National Freedom of Information Coalition found that 60% of its membership reported that open government litigation had "fallen dramatically" due to unavailability of funds.[95] An additional 85% reported they expected litigation would fall even more dramatically in the next three years.[96] While the FOIA Project found that FOIA lawsuits reached an all-time high in fiscal year 2014 only to increase in fiscal year 2015,[97] a study by the Project in 2013 found that news organizations filled fewer challenges in federal court for FOIA denials than in years past.[98] Thus, while there is more FOIA litigation, less of this litigation is being brought by members of the news media.

Commercial requesters are by far the greatest users of FOIA. As Professor Kwoka noted, commercial requesters "dominate the landscape at some agencies."[99] The the Coalition of Journalists for Open Government found that more than 60% of the requests their study sampled came from commercial interests, with 20% of those filed by professional data brokers.[100] Professor Kwoka also noted the most common users

---

[91] *Id.*

[92] Kwoka, *supra* note 12, at 1383.

[93] *Id.* at 1384 (writing that although Probes Reporter made no SEC FOIA requests, it advertises using FOIA requests to provide information to clients for "$1,187 per year for access to various FOIA requested records and reports, and [a higher level service] for $15,000 a year").

[94] *Id.* at 1388.

[95] *New Knight FOI Fund: Media Companies Involved in Fewer FOI Legal Actions*, NAT'L FREEDOM OF INFO. COALITION, Jan. 4, 2010, http://www.nfoic.org/new-knight-foi-fund.

[96] *Id.*

[97] David Burnham, FOIA *Lawsuits Reach Record High*, THE FOIA PROJECT, Jan. 6, 2016, http://foiaproject.org/2016/01/06/foia-lawsuits-reach-record-high/.

[98] *Media Making Fewer Challenges to Government Secrecy in Federal Court*, THE FOIA PROJECT, Mar. 14, 2013, http://foiaproject.org/2013/03/14/media-making-fewer-challenges-to-government-secrecy-in-federal-court/.

[99] Kowka, *supra* note 12, at 1365.

[100] *Frequent Filers, supra* note 60.

of FOIA were information resellers[101] and that at the SEC these users were filling "literally thousands of request per year."[102]

JOURNALISTS AND THE FOIA

Thus, while exact percentages are difficult to determine, it is clear that even though journalists were the intended users of FOIA and instrumental in its passage, the news media represent only a tiny fraction of the law's users. This leads to several questions about FOIA and the media. Why don't journalists use FOIA more? Even if they are not the top requesters, do journalists use FOIA *enough*? Are commercial requesters bad for FOIA, and do they impede its use by journalists?

The long delays associated with the law are a frequently cited reason for journalists not using FOIA.[103] As Melissa Davenport, director of the Washington, D.C., Open Government Coalition and Professor Kwoka wrote, "Information is often only as useful as it is timely."[104] Professor David Cuillier surveyed 445 U.S. journalists in 2010 to examine individual and institutional predictors or public records use.[105] Twelve percent of the journalists surveyed indicated they had used FOIA within the previous month, while 47% reported they had used the law at some point.[106] When journalists who did not use public records were asked why, 35% reported that they didn't know how to use access laws.[107] When asked specifically about FOIA, however, most journalists who did not use the law indicated it was specifically because of the length of time it took to receive records and that records were often redacted to the point of being useless.[108]

---

[101]Kowka, *supra* note 12, at 1379-1414 (discussing commercial requests at the SEC, FDA, EPA, DLA, FTC and NIH).

[102]*Id.* at 1423.

[103]*See, e.g.*, Michael Doyle, *Missed Information: The Reporting Tool That Reporters Don't Use*, WASH. MONTHLY, May 2000, at 38 (contending journalists don't use FOIA is because agencies take such a long time to respond to requests for information that the information is stale).

[104]Melissa Davenport & Margaret B. Kwoka, *Good But Not Great: Improving Access to Public Records Under the D.C. Freedom of Information Act*, 13 D.C. L. REV. 359, 386 (2010).

[105]David Cuillier, Pressed for Time: U.S. Journalists' Use of Public Records During Economic Crisis, at 9, paper presented at the Global Conference on Transparency Research, Newark, N.J., May 18-20, 2011.

[106]*Id.* at 13.

[107]*Id.*

[108]*Id.*

Although FOIA contains a twenty-day deadline for an agency to respond to a request,[109] it is well documented that FOIA requesters frequently face long delays. In fiscal year 2015, there were 713,168 FOIA requests,[110] down slightly from FY 2014, when there were 714,231 requests.[111] During FY 2015, the federal government processed 769,903 requests.[112] This was a 19% increase from FY 2014.[113] At the end of FY 2015, there was a backlog of 102,828 requests, a 35.6% decrease from FY 2014.[114] The Office of Information Policy directly attributed[115] this reduction in backlogged requests to a 2012 order that every year that "all agencies should make it a priority to close their ten oldest pending requests and appeals each year."[116]

For reporting purposes, agencies are directed to separate requests into three categories or "tracks": simple, complex and expedited.[117] Requests that "seek a high volume of material or require additional steps to process such as the need to search for records in multiple locations"[118] are categorized as "complex." Expedited track requests can be either simple or complex requests.[119] In FY 2015, the federal government received 7,353 requests for expedited processing,[120] granting 1,481 of them.[121] The average processing time for "simple track requests" was twenty-three days.[122] Although processing time for simple track requests had been decreasing steadily from FY 2010 to FY

[109] 5 U.S.C. § 552(a)(6)(A) (2012).

[110] U.S. DEPARTMENTT OF JUSTICE, SUMMARY OF ANNUAL FOIA REPORTS FOR FISCAL YEAR 2015, at 2 (2015), https://www.justice.gov/oip/reports/fy_2015_annual_foia_report_summary/download (hereinafter ANNUAL FOIA REPORTS FOR FISCAL YEAR 2015)

[111] *Id.* This represents a drop of less than one-tenth of 1%. The Department of Homeland Security received the most requests for the second straight year, although this number was down 3.5% from FY 2014. *Id.*

[112] *Id.* at 3.

[113] *Id.*

[114] *Id.* at 8. FY 2014 had an exceptionally high number of backlogged requests. In FY 2012, there were 71,790 backlogged requests. In FY 2013, there were 95,564. In FY 2014, there were 102,828. Rather than a vast improvement over historical numbers, FY 2015 numbers seem to simply be a return to previous levels with a slight increase from FY 2013. *Id.* at 9.

[115] *Id.* at 11.

[116] *OIP Guidance for Further Improvement*, U.S. DEPARTMENT OF JUSTICE, Aug. 15, 2014, https://www.justice.gov/oip/blog/foia-guidance-10.

[117] ANNUAL FOIA REPORTS FOR FISCAL YEAR 2015, *supra* note 109, at 13.

[118] *Id.* at 14.

[119] *Id.*

[120] *Id.* at 11.

[121] *Id.* at 12.

[122] *Id.* at 14.

2014, FY 2015 was an increase from FY 2014 of 2.5 days.[123] The average processing time for "complex requests," was much longer. In FY 2015, the average processing time for complex requests was 121.8 days,[124] an increase of 3.06 days from FY 2014.[125] Only five agencies were able to process complex requests in twenty or fewer days.[126] In FY 2015, the average processing times for expedited requests was 54.50 days,[127] a decrease of nearly fifty days from FY 2014 when the average processing time was 104.02 days.[128] The latest report by the FIOA Project, however, suggests wait times are increasing in 2016.[129]

Some journalists have suggested these delays and failures to find records are deliberate decisions by government bureaucrats.[130] Another explanation is that FOIA is an underfunded or unfunded mandate or that FOIA offices are simply being flooded with commercial requests and cannot keep up.[131] In FY 2015, the federal government employed 4,121.59[132] FOIA staff.[133] The total estimated cost of all FOIA related activities by the federal government in FY 2015 was $480.2 million.[134] In FY 2015, agencies collected a total $4.4 million dollars in FOIA fees, less than 1% of the total costs of FOIA.[135]

Another problem with journalists using FOIA is the way the law is written. FOIA directs federal agencies to "make records promptly available to any person."[136] FOIA does not provide journalists with analysis or answers to general queries, nor will FOIA officials research where information can be found. FOIA does not even require the government to affirmatively disclose information about what records it has. Thus, if

---

[123] *Id.* at 13. The average processing time was 28.34 days for FY 2010, 23.65 days for 2011, 22.66 days for FY 2012, 21.44 days for FY 2013, and 20.51 sayd for FY 2014. *Id.*

[124] *Id.* at 14.

[125] *Id.*

[126] *Id.*

[127] *Id.*

[128] *Id.*

[129] *Good News and Bad News On FOIA Responsiveness*, THE FOIA PROJECT, Jan. 26, 2016, http://foiaproject.org/2016/01/26/good-news-and-bad-news-on-foia-responsiveness/.

[130] *See, e.g.,* John Dyer, *50 Years of FOIA*, NIEMAN REPORTS, Winter 2016, at 40-41 (discussing journalists who have concluded that "FOIA is broken" because of the arbitrariness inherent in FOIA requests).

[131] *See* Kwoka, *supra* note 12, at 1422-24.

[132] ANNUAL FOIA REPORTS FOR FISCAL YEAR 2015, *supra* note 109, at 19. This number includes both full-time FOIA staff members and the cumulative percentages of the time spent on FOIA requests by personnel whose primary duties do not include FOIA.

[133] *Id.*

[134] *Id.* at 20.

[135] *Id.*

[136] 5 U.S.C. § 552(a)3(A)(2012).

a journalist does not know what records exist or what records to be looking for, FOIA is of little use. Requesters must have at least basic knowledge about the agency they are seeking information from to know what to ask for.[137] As journalist Shawn Boburg noted, in order to effectively request records, journalists need to understand how agencies work in order to "know what documents to look for."[138]

There are two solutions to this problem. First, the government should be more open about how records are kept. While Web sites like MuckRock[139] and FOIAmapper[140] can help a journalist discover what kinds of records can be requested and searchable databases of public information, the ultimate solution would be an online database maintained by each government agency of the types of records available. This sort of affirmative listing of documents would provide greater information to the public without requiring full disclosure of the information stored in the documents. Second, journalists who do not know what they are looking for need to craft more specific requests. For example, finding a source who can confirm or discuss a record can help journalists use FOIA better and confirm information given by a source. Discussing his use of FOIA, journalist Mark Feldstein explained that tips from sources allow him to narrow his focus or request a specific document.[141] As Feldstein summarized, "FOIA is a crude tool. Don't expect too much."[142]

Economics might also impact FOIA requests by members of the news media. As the U.S. news media have been fit with a historical decline in profits,[143] some commentators have worried that economic constraints may limit both FOIA requests and challenges to FOIA denials.[144]

[137]*See* Jennifer Shkabatur, *Transparency With(out) Accountability: Open Government in the United States*, 31 YALE L. & POL'Y REV. 79, 89-90 (2012).

[138]Dyer, *supra* note 129, at 43.

[139]Muckrock "is a non-profit, collaborative news site that brings together journalists, researchers, activists, and regular citizens to request, analyze, and share government documents, making politics more transparent and democracies more informed." About MuckRock, https://www.muckrock.com/about/. In addition to conducting original investigative reporting using government documents the site maintains a repository of original government records and information on how to file FOI requests. *Id.*

[140]FOIAmaper provides users with a searchable database of all information obtained by the site *via* FOIA requests. FOIAmapper Q & A, https://foiamapper.com/questions/.

[141]Stephanie Martinez, *The Good, the Bad, the Ugly of Using FOIA*, AM. JOURNALISM REV., Oct. 8, 2014, *available at* http://ajr.org/2014/10/08/foia-request-challenges/.

[142]*Id.*

[143]*See* Pew Research Center's Project for Excellence in Journalism, State of the News Media 2016, June 15, 2016, http://www.journalism.org/2016/06/15/state-of-the-news-media-2016/ (noting, "Average weekday newspaper circulation, print and digital combined, fell another 7% in 2015, the greatest decline since 2010. . . . In 2015, total advertising revenue among publicly traded companies declined nearly 8%, including losses not just in print, but digital as well").

[144]*See, e.g.*, Michelle Rydell, *No Money to Fight*, QUILL, Sept.-Oct. 2009, at 34.

Professor Cuillier's research focused the use of FOIA by journalists during economic crisis.[145] He found that journalists with the most experience were the most likely to use FOIA.[146] This led Professor Cuillier to worry that as news rooms continue to suffer economic loses and "buy out or lay off more experienced, costly journalists they lose the staff members" most likely to use FOIA.[147]

Litigating denials is also both costly and time consuming, additional barriers to access.[148] Professor Seth Kreimer noted media organizations might engage in a cost-benefits analysis when pursuing FOIA litigation. He wrote, "[O]nly news organizations sufficiently large to allow speculative investigation and expenditure of attorney's fees that might bring reputational gains in the medium-term future are likely to undertake the expenditures necessary to bring FOIA effectively to bear."[149] As one author noted, the appeal process at both the state and local level for access denials is "often impractical or impossible — especially for smaller newspapers."[150] Professor Clay Calvert noted this might be the biggest problem with the media's use of FOIA, noting, FOIA is "meaningless in practice" if the financial resources are not available to fight the time-consuming battles when requests are denied.[151]

Another worry is that privacy concerns are keeping FOIA officials from releasing information to journalists that would be valuable in writing stories. Because journalists frequently are interested in writing about people, some apparently believe FOIA is not worth using because the government goes overboard to protect personal information unless a waiver is signed. A major concern is that as government increasingly gathers personal information and better understands how much can be gleaned from that information, government officials are increasingly reluctant to share personal information with journalists.[152] Professor Jane Kirtley cited privacy as a significant concern, calling it "the biggest

---

[145]Cuillier, *supra* note 105.

[146]*Id.* at 17.

[147]*See id.*

[148]*See* Seth F. Kreimer, *The Freedom of Information Act and the Ecology of Transparency*, 10 U. PA. J. CONST. L. 1011, 1021-22 (2008) (citing numerous examples of lengthy and costly litigation of FOIA denials).

[149]*Id.* at 1023.

[150]Laura Danielson, *Giving Teeth to the Watchdog: Optimizing Open Records Appeals to Facilitate the Media's Use of FOIA Laws*, 2012 MICH. ST. L. REV. 981, 983.

[151]David L. Hudson Jr., *50 Years Later, Freedom of Information Act Still Chipping Away at Government's Secretive Culture*, ABAJOURNAL.COM, Jul. 1, 2016, http://www.abajournal.com/magazine/article/50th_anniversary_of_the_freedom_of_information_act/ (quoting Calvert).

[152]*See, e.g.*, Dyer, *supra* note 129, at 42 (discussing concerns with the government's unwillingness to release information because the government "know[s] so much about what can be gleaned from [personal] information").

obstacle to successful use of FOIA."[153] She contended that the concept of privacy has been expanded and distorted. Kirtley cited *National Archives and Records Administration v. Favish*,[154] a 2004 Supreme Court decision that broadly interpreted the personal privacy exemption in FOIA to include a right of familial or survivor privacy, as an example of how the concept of privacy has changed since FOIA was enacted.[155]

For these reasons, in some ways it is not surprising that commercial requesters are using FOIA more than journalists even if the law was primarily intended to benefit the news media. Commercial requesters typically look for information that is easier to find using FOIA, know what information they are looking for, and have advantages that stem from "the resources of business interests [and] their insider status as a repeat player in the process."[156] Because commercial requesters frequently are in the industry regulated by the agency from which they are seeking information, the commercial requester most likely has far greater knowledge of that industry than journalists and are thus more likely to to know what to ask for.[157] As Professor Kwoka noted, "[B]usinesses which use FOIA to further profit interest often meet all of the qualifications for effective requesters: they often have interest that are more long-term, not immediate in nature; they have resources; and the know enough about what they are looking for to effectively seek the information under FOIA."[158]

There is some debate about whether commercial requesters are harming the system. Melanie Ann Pustay, director of the Office of Information Policy at the Justice Department, blamed the delays on the large number of requests received by agencies from private citizens and corporations.[159] Professor Kwoka contended the majority of commercial requests are far from serving the goals of FOIA[160] and are "crowding out more publicly beneficial uses of FOIA."[161] Michael Morisy, co-founder of the news site MuckRock, however, believes that commercial requests help train FOIA officials at smaller agencies how to process requests and in the long run help journalists acquire

[153] Hudson, *supra* note 150 (quoting interview with Kirtley).

[154] 541 U.S. 157 (2003).

[155] Hudson, *supra* note 150 (quoting interview with Kirtley).

[156] Kwoka, *supra* note 12, at 1414.

[157] Shkabatur, *supra* note 136, at 89-90.

[158] Kwoka, *supra* note 12, at 1376.

[159] Ravi Somaiya, *A Wizard at Prying Government Secrets from the Government*, N.Y. TIMES, Jul. 19, 2015, *available at* http://www.nytimes.com/2015/07/20/business/a-wizard-at-prying-government-secrets-from-the-government.html.

[160] Kowka, *supra* note 12, at 1415.

[161] *Id.* at 1422.

information.[162] While Kwoka argued commercial requesters are damaging "FOIA's democratic aspirations,"[163] rather than limiting commercial requesters or giving journalists a preferred position she advocated for greater affirmative government disclosure.[164] It is also important to note that commercial use of FOIA is not improper. Although FOIA was written with the news media in mind, it clearly applies to everyone. Even Professor Kwoka notes that commercial requests are not "undesirable," she simply worries that the volume of commercial requests are hurting media requests given the economic constraints of most FOIA offices.[165]

Even if news media requests are small compared to commercial requests, it is still important to note these requests frequently result in compelling stories that do advance both the right to know and the ability of the press to work as a government watchdog. FOIA most certainly contributes to journalists' ability to keep the public informed and increase its understanding of government activities. In addition, some journalists suggest that the use of FOIA is increasing among members of the media and note the many great stories that come from FOIA despite problems with the law. Journalists, after all, cite public records in a fifth of their news stories.[166] Journalist Ravi Somaiya wrote that FOIA has gained new importance sine "the Obama administration has overseen a crackdown on government employees talking to journalists."[167] Jason Leopold, the so-called "FOIA terrorist" and contributor to Vice News, noted that even when government employees will talk they frequently require anonymity and using FOIA is a better alternative to citing an anonymous source.[168] Morisy believes that several high profile stories that have attributed the information in the article to FOIA requests has renewed interest in FOIA.[169] Morisy, who does news room training on how to use FOIA across the country, also noted that during these trainings, more and more journalists now indicate they are comfortable doing FOIA requests than in years past.[170] There is also evidence that new media organizations are using FOIA at greater rates

[162]Telephone interview with Michael Morisy (Jun. 23, 2016).

[163]Kowka, *supra* note 12, at 1427.

[164]*Id.* at 1429-33.

[165]*Id.* at 1436.

[166]*Open Doors: FOI and Daily News Coverage*, SOCIETY OF PROFESSIONAL JOURNALISTS (last visited Jun. 28, 2016), http://www.spj.org/opendoors5.asp.

[167]Somaiya, *supra* note 158.

[168]Rose Creasman Welcom, *Meet Vice News's Jason Leopold, the "FOIA Terrorist,"* AM. J. REV. Dec. 23, 2014, *available at* http://ajr.org/2014/12/23/meet-vices-jason-leopold-foia-terrorist/(quoting interview with Leopold).

[169]Interview with Morisy, *supra* note 169.

[170]*Id.*

than traditional news organizations and are engaging in a sort of FOIA carpet bombing that frequently results in a great deal of data.[171]

Morisy also noted that there are a large number of powerful stories that have used FOIA. "When we started MuckRock we read a lot of Pulitzer Prize winning stories. The thing that many of them had in common, besides great storytelling, was the use of public records," he said.[172] For example, the 2014 Pulitzer Prize winning "Other than Honorable" series used FOIA requests to the U.S. Army to gather information about Army personnel suffering from Post-Traumatic Stress Disorder who were given so-called Chapter 10 discharges and lost their veterans benefits in lieu of facing a court-martials.[173] Other authors have also noted that ability of FOI laws to facilitate watchdog journalism, such as the use of state freedom of information laws to reveal corruption by Detroit Mayor Kwame Kilpatrick.[174]

In addition, journalists routinely use information provided by nonprofit organizations, government watchdog groups, and other organizations that were obtained *via* FOIA requests.[175] Professor Seth F. Kreimer noted that some of the most effective requesters are well-financed nonprofits. Professor Kreimer's list of "most effective requesters" included the National Security Archives, the American Civil Liberties Union, the Electronic Privacy Information Center, the Electronic Frontier Foundation, the Center for Constitutional Rights, Judicial Watch, and the Center for National Security Studies[176] – organizations that frequently work with the news media to disseminate information on government activities. Others have noted the true benefit of FOIA is that it has fostered greater openness in government. As Professor Kirtly noted, "I don't think it is possible to overstate the impact of FOIA on openness in government."[177]

---

[171]A search of FOIA logs assembled by FOIAmapper.com for the term "MuckRock" returned 993 results for requests made by the organization.

[172]Interview with Morisy, *supra* note 169.

[173]*See Other Than Honorable*, THE GAZETTE, *available at* http://cdn.csgazette.biz/soldiers/. *See also*, Dyer, *supra* note 129, at 38-39 (calling FOIA the "linchpin" of the series and discussing the process which lead to the authors decision to use FOIA to gather information for the story); *The FOIA Files*, THE SUNSHINE IN GOVERNMENT INITIATIVE, http://sunshineingovernment.org/wordpress/the-foia-files/ (last visited Jul. 1, 2016)(catalog of more than 700 stories using information obtained *via* FOIA).

[174]Danielson, *supra* note 149, at 981-82 (2012) (describing the use of open records laws to obtain information and noting the story "amply demonstrates the importance of open records laws for government transparency and accountability").

[175]*See* Kreimer, *supra* note 148, at 1024.

[176]*Id.*

[177]Hudson, *supra* note 150.

CONCLUSION

FOIA was designed to advance First Amendment ideals related to self-government and the watchdog function of the press. It was designed by journalists and their allies in Congress to be a tool of democracy. However, it is clear that news media representatives constitute a small minority of requesters. While exact numbers are difficult if not impossible to ascertain, it's clear that fewer than one tenth of FOIA requests are filed by journalists. However, based on the numerous and important stories that have come from FOIA requests, it is equally clear that it is a valuable tool for journalists reporting on a wide range of topics. Journalists like Morisy have an optimism that is contagious when discussing FOIA. It is hard to not be swayed by his enthusiasm and to believe that despite its flaws and limits, many journalists find FOIA to be an effective tool for gathering information. Despite this optimism, however, both FOIA itself and the way journalists use it could be improved. Decreasing delays and providing information about what kinds of information is available would certainly help improve FOIA, while increased training on how to use FOIA and education on the many powerful stories that have been creating using data obtained by the law would increase its use by journalists.

BRINGING BACK FULL DISCLOSURE: A CALL FOR DISMANTLING FOIA

DAXTON R. "CHIP" STEWART
CHARLES N. DAVIS

The Freedom of Information Act began as a tool for ensuring full disclosure of federal government agencies, but it has consistently failed to live up to these expectations. Despite frequent amendments, FOIA remains a law rooted in an era of paper record-keeping, where files are created and stored by government, protected from release by decades of judicial expansion of exemptions, and remain largely hidden from public scrutiny. Modern computing technology should allow much easier and broader access for citizens, but FOIA needs radical transformation to reclaim its purpose. This article calls for a structural overhaul of FOIA focusing on proactive transparency, taking advantage of modern record-keeping technology such as open government portals and automation to enable citizen access to records as early as possible. Exceptions should be narrow and applied at the moment a record is created, and incentives should shift to favor disclosure in the face of agency inaction or delay.

Before he was appointed to the Supreme Court of the United States, Antonin Scalia lambasted the federal Freedom of Information Act, calling it "the Taj Mahal of the Doctrine of Unanticipated Consequences" that was "a far cry from John Q. Public finding out how his government works."[1] Justice Scalia was right, albeit for reasons wholly unrelated to his arguments at the time. He recognized that in the two decades since it had become law in 1966, FOIA had become a lumbering beast, a tool

[1]Antonin Scalia, *The Freedom of Information Act Has No Clothes*, 6 AEI J. ON GOV'T & SOC'Y 14, 15-16 (1986). Scalia was skeptical of FOIA in general, seeing it as overly burdensome in terms of both financial costs and interference with good governance and writing that it was a "romantic notion" that the executive branch could be kept in check through "do-it-yourself oversight by the public and, its surrogate, the press." *Id.* at 19.

for corporate lawyers, and a burden on the justice system that did little to serve its purpose as the "ultimate guarantee of responsible government."[2] FOIA is now fifty years old, and despite several efforts to revise and update the law, it still has not delivered on its promise to assure transparency of federal government agencies. The purpose of FOIA was to enable the "fullest possible disclosure"[3] of government records, and yet, half a century later, obfuscation and delay are the hallmarks of a law that was supposed to ensure the people's right to know. In 2016, a House of Representatives oversight committee reviewing the FOIA issued a final report simply titled *FOIA is Broken*.[4] Broken? Perhaps. A more accurate description might be petrified.

Among citizens and journalists trying to use FOIA to shed light on government activities, horror stories abound.[5] It took more than four years for Sulome Anderson, the daughter of former hostage Terry Anderson, to get access to documents about his kidnapping, many heavily redacted, from twenty years earlier.[6] Journalist Phil Eil, working on a book about a physician known as the "Pill Mill Doctor" who was convicted of illegally distributing pain medications in 2012, had after four years only received a fraction of the documents he requested under FOIA about evidence used in the highly-publicized federal trial, and most of those were unusable because they had been so heavily redacted.[7] The Transportation Safety Administration took seven years to respond to a FOIA request about misconduct by federal air marshals filed in 2008, covering up years of abuse.[8] Army officials deliberately delayed access to information about concussions at West Point, requested by *The New York Times*, while trying to spin a more

[2] *Id.* at 16.

[3] Martin Halstuk & Bill Chamberlin, *The Freedom of Information Act 1966-2006: A Retrospective on the Rise of Privacy Protection Over the Public Interest in Knowing What the Government's Up To*, 11 COMM. L. & POL'Y 511, 533 (2006).

[4] U.S. HOUSE OF REPRESENTATIVES COMMITTEE ON OVERSIGHT AND GOVERNMENT REFORM, FOIA IS BROKEN: A REPORT 39 (2016) (hereinafter FOIA IS BROKEN).

[5] "Every investigative journalist has a FOIA horror story or an instance in which powerful interests simply refused to play ball," wrote one critic. Sulome Anderson, *My Dad's Long, Frustrating Battle with the US Government to Learn About his Own Kidnapping*, VICE, June 5, 2015, https://www.vice.com/read/my-dads-long-frustrating-battle-with-the-us-government-to-learn-about-his-own-kidnapping-605 (last visited June 20, 2016).

[6] *See id.*

[7] *See id.* Luke O'Neil. *Why Is the DEA Not Cooperating with This FOIA Request*, ESQUIRE, Dec. 2, 2015, *available at* http://www.esquire.com/news-politics/a40126/phil-eil-dea-lawsuit/ (last visited June 20, 2016).

[8] *See id.* Michael Grabell, *The TSA Releases Data on Air Marshal Misconduct, 7 Years After We Asked*, PROPUBLICA, Feb. 24, 2016, https://www.propublica.org/article/tsa-releases-data-on-air-marshal-misconduct-7-years-after-we-asked (last visited June 20, 2016).

positive story to other media outlets, repeating a tactic the Army had successfully deployed regarding requests about injured veterans the previous year.[9] And Jason Leopold, who one government agency dubbed the "FOIA Terrorist" for his requests as a journalist for Vice News,[10] has had to go to court to force the Pentagon to disclose just the titles of reports in its database, and even then, the Department of Defense said it would only cooperate "as long as you promise to never file a FOIA request again."[11]

How did FOIA become a tool for preserving secrecy rather than transparency, and what can be done about it? In this article, we examine the mechanics of FOIA, which was drafted and enacted with good intentions but wound up doing little to advance the transparency failures that had arisen under the old Administrative Procedure Act it was supposed to replace. The APA, mocked by access advocates for predicating access on an agency's determination that it was in the public interest or otherwise could be denied for "good cause found,"[12] was replaced by a statute that has grown equally ineffective over time, its requirements ossified by decades of litigation, and layer upon layer of judicial interpretation rending the plain meaning of the statute meaningless.

Structural problems have plagued the law from the start, requiring frequent amendments and updates. Times have changed, and technology has transformed the way records are kept and managed, though FOIA has had problems keeping pace, rooted in the paper-first mindset of the era in which it was initially drafted. Of course paper records were the only option when FOIA was passed in 1966, and that technology, by necessity, kept the records in the hands of government until they were requested and copies had to be made. In this sense, a record was only open and available when an agency determined it to be so, and even then, only when it determined that following the requirements of FOIA was suitable in that situation, with little practical consequence for noncompliance. Additionally, what were initially intended to be narrow exemptions to FOIA have been judicially enlarged in some instances to the point of absurdity.

---

[9]*See* Dave Phillips, *Generals Sought More Positive Coverage on Head Injuries, Document Shows*, N.Y. TIMES, Sept. 30, 2015, at A15.

[10]Michael Morisy, *Reporter's Voice: Jason Leopold*, MUCKROCK, July 12, 2013, https://www.muckrock.com/news/archives/2013/jul/12/jason-leopold-foia-terrorist-shares-his-transparen/ (last visited June 20, 2016).

[11]Erik Wemple, *Judge Orders Release of Pentagon Records in Jason Leopold FOIA Case*, WASH. POST, June 11, 2015, *available at* https://www.washingtonpost.com/blogs/erik-wemple/wp/2015/06/11/judge-orders-release-of-pentagon-records-in-jason-leopold-foia-case/ (last visited June 20, 2016).

[12]H.R. Rep. No. 89-1497, 22-23 (1966).

In response to continued public criticism about government transparency, Congress and the executive branch have made serious efforts, through legislation and policy directives, to correct some of the flaws of FOIA and to respond to the advance of computer record-keeping, such as the passage of E-FOIA in 1996,[13] President Barack Obama's Open Government Directive in 2009,[14] and enactment of a new round of amendments in 2016.[15] However, by resting on the flawed design of FOIA legislation drafted in a different era, these and other responses continue to fall short. Process-oriented reforms are laudatory but mask the real problem with FOIA – its content. The act has reached the point of no return, in need of systemic, top-to-bottom reform, rather than the piecemeal, process-oriented reforms that have typified legislative action on FOIA since the 1970s.

Records still largely begin their lives as closed and secret, with major effort required by citizens to gain access, at the discretion of government agencies. Consider the pilot project headed up by the Office of Information Policy entitled "Release to One, Release to All," under which federal agencies would host the documents they released pursuant to FOIA requests on their Web sites so they would be available to anyone.[16] This policy, while plausibly advancing transparency goals, starts from the flawed premise that government records are only actually available to the public upon request and release. That process, the original sin of FOIA that instantly undermines the presumption of openness intended by Congress when the law was passed in 1966, must be replaced with a digital counterpart that presumes openness as a starting point. Modern technology allows for more radical, proactive openness, where records are open instantly and available to the public that has paid for their creation, without the permission of government officials required.

The House Oversight Committee, in the conclusion of its *FOIA is Broken* report, said the law had become "unacceptably neutered," and noted, "Structural reform is necessary to ensure the FOIA tool works as intended."[17] The purpose of this article is to consider what "struc-

[13]Electronic Freedom of Information Act Amendments of 1996, Pub. L. No. 104-231 (1996).

[14]Office of Mgmt. & Budget, Exec. Office of the President, Open Government Directive (Dec. 8, 2009).

[15]FOIA Improvement Act of 2016, Pub. Law No. 114-185 (2016).

[16]*See* Alexander Howard, *With "Release to One, Release to All," U.S. Pilots New Freedom of Information Policy*, Huffington Post, July 20, 2015, http://www.huffingtonpost.com/entry/with-release-to-one-release-to-all-us-pilots-new-freedom-of-information-policy_us_559f1661e4b05b1d0290135b (last visited June 20, 2016).

[17]FOIA is Broken, *supra* note 4, at 39.

tural reform" would look like if we were to dismantle FOIA and start again, from scratch, with an understanding of how records are created and maintained in the digital age.

BACKGROUND

When FOIA was enacted in 1966, the law clearly was intended as a means for ensuring transparency, with narrow exemptions only applied to protect the most sensitive information held by government agencies. In spite of this, FOIA has failed to live up to its promise of transparency, with agencies broadly applying exemptions and federal courts enabling expansion of the scope of these exemptions, typically in the name of protecting privacy. The failure of FOIA to serve its intended purpose can be traced back to its first decade as law, as expanded government record-keeping and privacy concerns about computers created obstacles for transparency.

Full Disclosure: The Purpose of FOIA

Fifty years ago, citizens faced many of the same hurdles they do today when trying to access federal agency records. Witnesses testifying before a House committee in 1965 said that the Administrative Procedure Act, which included a section requiring disclosure of agency records, had "been used more as an excuse for withholding than as a disclosure statute," and the committee found that the APA "was being used as an excuse for secrecy."[18] In 1966, as Congress began considering the bill that became FOIA, it noted the weaknesses of the APA – particularly in allowing broad agency discretion to deny access based on the "public interest" or otherwise "required for good cause" – and clearly stated that the purpose of the new law would be "to eliminate such phrases" and "to establish a general philosophy of full agency disclosure."[19] President Lyndon B. Johnson, in a statement upon signing the bill, recognized that "freedom of information is so vital that only the national security, not the whim of public officials, should determine when it must be restricted."[20]

By 1974, with public trust in government waning on the heels of Watergate, it was clear that FOIA was not living up to its intended purpose. It had instead become, in practice, a "'freedom from information'

[18]H.R. Rep. No. 89-813, 38 (1965).

[19]89 Cong. Rec. S26821 (Oct. 13, 1965).

[20]Presidential Statement upon Signing S.1160 (July 4, 1966).

law," as a Senate committee noted, with an average delay of thirty-three days for agency responses to requests, excessive copying fees, and a "cumbersome and costly legal remedy" for those who have to go to court after having been denied access.[21] Representative Bill Alexander from Arkansas recounted an effort by a public interest group seeking documents about pesticides from the Department of Agriculture, which were initially denied, then ordered by a court to be released, but even then, the department said it would "cost $91,000 and take a year and a half to get it together."[22] The amendments, he said, were intended to "put an end to the ridiculous delays, excuses, and bureaucratic runarounds which have denied U.S. citizens the 'right to know' and made Americans a captive of their own Government."[23] Congress tried to tighten up the exemptions and also tried to pass sanctions that included sixty-day suspensions for federal agency employees who were found to deny access to records without a "reasonable basis in law." President Gerald Ford, House members, and government employee unions opposed the severity of those sanctions, so the bill was watered down to make punishment only after both a court finding that the denial was done "arbitrarily or capriciously" and after a disciplinary hearing was conducted against the employee.[24] Even then, Congress had to override a presidential veto to pass the FOIA amendments, with senators using passionate language in favor of government transparency and accountability. Senator Walter Mondale, describing increased secrecy and federal agency cover-ups, saw the 1974 amendments as a reaffirmation of the government's commitment to transparency, as was the hope of FOIA: "The American people are tired of the politics of secrecy. They are demanding a politics of honesty and openness. [The amendments] will be an important step in restoring the faith of a free people in their Government."[25]

Even then, agencies and courts continued to undermine the clear intent favoring transparency. In 1975, in *Administrator, FAA v. Robertson*, the Supreme Court ignored this intent, instead finding "broad, flexible discretion" to agencies regarding application of exemptions, requiring a new round of clarification of the purpose of the law.[26] Congress "reiterated its policy of full disclosure" in 1976, when it narrowed the scope of Exemption 3 in response to the ruling.[27] The

[21] S. Rep. 93-854, 155 (1974).

[22] 120 Cong. Rec. H10001, 388 (Oct. 7, 1974).

[23] *Id.*

[24] *Id.* at 376-80.

[25] 120 Cong. Rec. S19806, 472-73 (Nov. 21, 1974).

[26] 422 U.S. 255, 267 (1975).

[27] Halstuk & Chamberlin, *supra* note 3, at 535.

pattern, however, was established: congressional proclamation, followed by judicial retreat.

Despite the amendments to FOIA that continuously sought to expand public access and uphold the promise of full government agency transparency, delays and frustration persisted. A House committee examining the first twenty years of FOIA in 1986 found "inadequate resources, unnecessary bureaucratic complexity, political interference with the disclosure process, poor organization of agency records, and a lack of commitment by agencies to disclosure" as weaknesses in the act.[28] These weaknesses were due, at least in part, to the ways in which records were created and managed by agencies. And if anything, they have worsened, exacerbated by the digital age.

The Emergence of Computer Record-Keeping

When Congress began considering FOIA in the mid-1960s, with computing in its infancy, records were kept primarily on paper.[29] While the federal government had been using computers as early as ENIAC by the Army in 1945 and UNIVAC for the census in 1951, these computers were largely used for calculation and scientific problem-solving; by 1965, about two-thirds of the nearly 2,200 computers used by the federal government were in the Department of Defense, assigned to tasks such as "missile simulation, test(ing) data reduction, and war gaming," while many of the others were employed by NASA to aid in calculations for space missions.[30]

By the early 1970s, computers were being used more frequently by the government in areas such as tax, Social Security, criminal, and health records. A committee assembled by the U.S. Department of Health, Education & Welfare responded to public concerns about the rise of computer record-keeping in a report in 1973 that called for establishment of "fair information practices," citing a public opinion survey that showed "worries and anxieties about computers and personal privacy" in about a third of those interviewed and fear of a "'Big Brother' system" in which intelligence is gathered and citizens lose control of information about themselves.[31] The committee was skeptical of "the so-called 'Freedom of Information Act,'" calling it "an instrument for

[28]H.R. Rep. 99-832 (1986) (cited in H.R. Rep. 104-795, 13 (1996)).

[29]H.R. Rep. 104-795, 11 (1996).

[30]James A. Ward, *The Impact of Computers on the Government*, 1965 AM. FED'N OF INFO. PROCESSING SOCIETIES 37, 38.

[31]U.S. DEP'T OF HEALTH, EDUC. & WELFARE, COMPUTERS AND THE RIGHTS OF CITIZENS 29 (1973).

disclosing information rather than for balancing the conflicting interests that surround the public disclosure and use of personal records."[32] One recommendation of the committee was an amendment to FOIA that would require agencies to obtain consent from individuals before disclosing personally-identifiable information contained in government databases.[33] While Congress did not specifically amend FOIA in this way, it did follow several of the committee's recommendations in passing the Federal Privacy Act in 1974.[34]

Federal agencies' use of computers advanced significantly over the next decade, and by 1985, a committee studying government recordkeeping estimated that there were "over 200,000 personal computers now in use at all levels of government."[35] However, the transition to electronic record-keeping was still in its infancy, and there was little consistency within the federal government on how records were created and stored. Most records were still kept as paper documents, and the culture of record-keeping was still rooted in paper: "Significantly, the habits developed by office personnel rely almost entirely on paper documentation. Records management has meant paper management.. .. The detailed manuals on filing procedures, correspondence control, and records scheduling are primarily concerned with paper files."[36]

By 1990, more than 48,000 large mainframe computers and more than a million personal computers in use in federal agencies, yet commentators noted the "low priority placed on public access in the design of government computer systems."[37] Concerns about security breaches and cost, as well as the wide variety of technology in use that made standardization nearly impossible, were also holding back public access to government records.[38] It had become clear that FOIA, drafted in the era of paper records, would need to be updated to address the widespread growth of electronic record-keeping by federal agencies, while also harnessing the power of computers and the emerging Internet to serve the core purposes of FOIA. As a House committee considering amendments to the law noted: "The FOIA must stay abreast of these developments in order to ensure continued public access to

[32]*Id.* at 35.

[33]*Id.* at xxvii.

[34]Privacy Act of 1974, Pub. L. No. 93-579 (1974).

[35]COMMITTEE ON THE RECORDS OF GOVERNMENT, REPORT (1985).

[36]*Id.* at 26.

[37]Matthew D. Bunker, Sigman L. Splichal, Bill F. Chamberlin & Linda M. Perry, *Access to Government-Held Information in the Computer Age: Applying Legal Doctrine to Emerging Technology*, 20 FLA. ST. L. REV. 543, 559-60 (1993).

[38]*Id.* at 564 (citing U.S. OFFICE OF TECH'Y ASSESSMENT, INNOVATIVE USE OF INFORMATION TECHNOLOGY FACILITATING PUBLIC ACCESS TO AGENCY DECISIONMAKING: AN ASSESSMENT OF THE EXPERIENCE IN STATE AND LOCAL GOVERNMENTS (1985)).

Government information. The FOIA must promote uniformity among agencies, reduce uncertainty among FOIA requestors, and avoid potential disagreements between the two."[39] Again, while considering these amendments to FOIA, Congress noted that "full disclosure of information to the public" is "critical to maintaining an open and free society."[40] The resulting legislation was the Electronic Freedom of Information Act of 1996, which required agencies to (1) formally extend FOIA to cover records in electronic formats; (2) create an electronic reading room where people can access "copies of all records, regardless of form or format," which have been released pursuant to a request and are likely to become the subject of similar requests in the future; and (3) provide records "in any form or format requested by the person" to the extent that the records are "readily reproducible" in that format.[41]

While the use of computers in federal agencies continued to expand, records continued to be kept in hodgepodge fashion, and FOIA compliance remained problematic. In 2005, a survey of federal agencies showed that while many agencies were making concerted efforts to move toward keeping and managing electronic records, "[T]he majority of all organizations still designate paper as their official record-keeping format," using a dual system that used both paper and digital records.[42] Even the dual system, however, could not handle issues such as email,[43] a problem that had been anticipated for almost fifteen years by this point.[44] In a little less than a decade after E-FOIA was passed, the report found, "[M]any organizations are still puzzled over how to deal with the management of electronic records," with federal agencies placing low priority on such matters, and employees showing little understanding of how electronic record-keeping worked.[45]

Today, the executive branch widely acknowledges the move toward effective computer record keeping, with the Obama administration calling for agencies to "commit immediately to the transition to a digital government" in 2012.[46] The administration's directive called for all permanent records to be managed in electronic format by 2019, and for all

[39]H.R. Rep. 104-795, 12 (1996).

[40]*Id.* at 7.

[41]Electronic Freedom of Information Amendments of 1996, Pub. L. No. 104-231 (1996).

[42]Lee Stickland, Best Practices in Electronic Records Management: A Survey and Report on Federal Government Agencies' Record Keeping Policies and Practices 1 (2005).

[43]*Id.* at 2.

[44]*See* Bunker et al., *supra* note 37, at 595-98.

[45]Stickland, *supra* note 42, at 3.

[46]Office of Mgmt. & Budget, Exec. Office of the President, Managing Government Records Directive 3 (Aug. 24, 2012).

email records to be managed in an electronic system with capabilities to "identify, retrieve, and retain" email records.[47] We are in an age where federal agency documents are almost entirely generated through some sort of electronic device – whether on a government or personal computer or on a smartphone – rather than on paper. Miriam Nisbet, the first director of the FOIA ombuds program in the Office of Government Information Services, noted in 2012, "With the FOIA as a backdrop, and fueled by technological development, the government has the ability now – more than ever – to make its records available to the governed (that is, the public) without waiting for a request to be made under the FOIA."[48]

And yet, despite the tools available, and an almost complete transition to digital management of records, FOIA compliance is still so troublesome and riddled with abuse and delays as to require regular overhauls, including a new round of amendments required to fix the "broken" law as it neared its fiftieth anniversary. Why, after half a century, does FOIA continue to fall short of its framers' intent of "full disclosure"? Besides the aforementioned structural issues and inadequate responses to technological change, the courts have further watered down FOIA through its interpretations of what were initially intended to be very narrow exemptions.

Privacy Exceptionalism and Exemption Expansion

An agency must disclose any record that does not fall within one of the nine categories of information exempted from disclosure under the act.[49] The nine exemptions provide example after example of the practical stagnation of the law, as the courts have wrestled with ambiguous legislative language, limiting the law's coverage in ways that debilitate its effectiveness.

Generally, Congress intended the exemptions to protect against disclosure of information that would substantially harm national defense or foreign policy, individual privacy interests, business proprietary interests, and the efficient operation of governmental functions. Agencies have had the authority to construe the exemptions as discretionary rather than mandatory when no harm would result from disclosure of the requested information.[50] If a requested document falls within one of

[47] *Id.*

[48] Miriam Nisbet, Openness: Are We There Yet (And How Will We Know)?, 1, presentation for the International Conference on Archives, Brisbane, Australia (2012).

[49] 5 U.S.C. § 552(b)(1)-(9) (2016).

[50] *See* Chrysler Corp. v. Brown, 441 U.S. 281, 293 (1979).

the nine exemptions, the agency can release it anyway as an exercise of its discretionary powers. Moreover, "These exemptions are specifically made exclusive ... and must be narrowly construed."[51]

Would that they were. Instead, fifty years of litigation under the act have resulted in several exemptions being eviscerated by judicial interpretations undermining earlier pronouncements of narrow construction. As Martin Halstuk, Benjamin Cramer and Michael Todd noted in a 2014 study, the Supreme Court had heard eight cases involving FOIA exemptions and privacy, and had sided with the government in all but one case, leading to what the authors called the doctrine of "privacy exceptionalism" for a law intended to promote transparency, rather than its opposite.[52]

Consider Exemption 2, for example, which allows agencies to withhold documents "related solely to internal personnel rules and practices." In one of the first substantive treatments of the act, the Supreme Court in 1976 described the exemption as one designed "to relieve agencies of the burden of assembling and maintaining for public inspection matter in which the public could not reasonably be expected to have an interest."[53]

Later, courts identified a smaller subset of records covered by the exemption, records that might be exempt if its disclosure would risk circumvention of law or agency regulations. In order to fall into this category, the material will normally have to regulate internal agency conduct rather than public behavior.[54]

From that rather concise reading, future courts have greatly expanded the exemption to cover records pertaining to law enforcement, national security and other records far from its original purview.[55] Exemption 2's tortured legislative history (featuring dueling House and Senate reports, with the Senate's interpretation of the exemption much more crabbed than the House's)[56] fueled the diminution of the statute's plain meaning. In *Crooker v. Bureau of Alcohol, Tobacco & Firearms*, the United States Circuit Court for the District of Columbia held that a Bureau of Alcohol, Tobacco and Firearms agent training manual was exempt from disclosure under Exemption 2 despite its obvious interest

---

[51]Dept. of the Air Force v. Rose, 425 U.S. 352, 361 (1976).

[52]Martin E. Halstuk, Benjamin W. Cramer & Michael E. Todd, *Tipping the Scales: How the U.S. Supreme Court Eviscerated Freedom of Information in Favor of Privacy*, *in* CHARLES N. DAVIS & DAVID CUILLIER (EDS), TRANSPARENCY 2.0 20 (2014).

[53]*See* 425 U.S. at 369.

[54]*See* Church of Scientology v. Smith, 721 F.2d 828, 830-31 n.4 (D.C. Cir. 1983).

[55]*See* Marnie J. Carro, *Crooker v. Bureau of Alcohol, Tobacco & Firearms: A Result-Oriented Approach to FOIA Exemption 2*, 32 CATH. U. L. REV. 317 (1983).

[56]*See id.* at 318-19.

to some members of the public.[57] The court reasoned that the exemption permits the nondisclosure of information that relates predominantly to the internal workings of an agency that are not the subject of any substantial, valid public interest. Therefore, it concluded that Exemption 2 applies if the information requested meets a test of "predominant internality" and its disclosure would pose a significant risk of circumvention of agency law.[58]

What had been treated largely as an exemption for "housekeeping" records[59] quickly became far more, as the Second Circuit created a judicial rationale for enlarging the scope of Exemption 2 in *Caplan v. Bureau of Alcohol, Tobacco & Firearms*.[60] The court withheld disclosure of a Bureau of Alcohol, Tobacco and Firearms manual dealing with raids and searches. The court reasoned that in situations in which disclosure would risk physical harm to law enforcement personnel, precedent did not foreclose adopting the House report's more narrow interpretation of Exemption 2, and concluded that a reading of both the House and Senate reports on the pertinent subsections (b)(2) and (a)(2)(C) provided evidence of an intent that the manual be withheld on the basis of Exemption 2.[61] Therefore, the court held that Exemption 2 exempts from disclosure internal agency matters where disclosure might risk circumvention of agency law.[62]

Only a couple of years later, the Ninth Circuit, in *Hardy v. Bureau of Alcohol, Tobacco & Firearms,* held that portions of the Bureau of Alcohol, Tobacco and Firearms manual dealing with raids and searches were exempt from disclosure because they were "law enforcement materials, disclosure of which may risk circumvention of agency regulations."[63] The court reviewed the other two approaches used by the circuits to exempt law enforcement materials and rejected the approach taken by courts as unfaithful to the structure of FOIA, which requires full disclosure except in the case of a specific exemption. The court asserted that earlier decisions did not foreclose reliance on the House report to use Exemption 2 to withhold materials that could aid in the circumvention of the law.[64]

Thus, when the D.C. Circuit attempted to make order of Exemption 2 in *Crooker*, the precedent was sufficiently divergent that its best efforts

[57] 670 F.2d 1051 (D.C. Cir. 1981).
[58] *Id.* at 1074.
[59] Cox v. United States Dep't of Justice, 576 F.2d 1302, 1309 (8th Cir. 1978).
[60] 587 F.2d 544 (2d Cir. 1978).
[61] *Id.* at 547.
[62] *Id.* at 548.
[63] 631 F.2d 653, 657 (9th Cir. 1980).
[64] *Id.*

only made matters worse. As one commentator noted, "[T]he extent to which *Crooker* manipulated the wording, legislative history, and case law on exemption 2 is unique."[65] The result was almost preordained: The majority's reliance on a narrow reading of the exemption emanating from the House report and never embodied in an amendment to the exemption, the intent found by the majority reflects no more than the wishes of some of the opponents of the act in the House at the time, and in no way reconciles the competing Senate report on the bill. Its result, driven by judicial expression of congressional intent, resulted in a watering down of the plain meaning of the statute. While the Supreme Court has narrowed the construction of exemptions in recent years,[66] it is easy to remain skeptical that agencies will make a move toward transparency when there are so few incentives for compliance.

Conflicting legislative intent, muddled through years of often irreconcilable precedent and finally, an attempt at clarity that becomes anything but: The treatment of Exemption 2 is a lens upon which one could similarly discuss Exemption 4 (trade secrets), Exemption 6 (personal privacy) and Exemption 7 (law enforcement). Each of the major FOIA exemptions has been criticized as flawed in execution on much the same grounds. The legal framework has turned what was supposed to be a broad presumption in favor of full disclosure into a patchwork of judicially created exemptions layered on top of legislatively created exemptions, with three notorious ones identified by FOIA scholars Martin Halstuk and Bill Chamberlin:[67] (1) Minimal privacy concerns for non-intimate matters such as citizenship status and passport information contained in records are enough to trigger non-disclosure under Exemption 6, which was to have "broad, rather than a narrow meaning" to protect privacy;[68] (2) allowing withholding records under Exemption 7(c) for materials that do not fall within the "central purpose" of FOIA, which the Court defined as ensuring that the government's activities are open to public scrutiny, disregarding legislative history supporting the opposite of this;[69] and (3) creating a new hurdle requiring requesters seeking records about potential government wrongdoing

[65] *See* Carro, *supra* note 55, at 340.

[66] *See* Milner v. Dep't. of Navy, 562 U.S. 562 (2011) (holding that an agency's use of Exemption 2 for "personnel and rules and practices" could not validly be used to exempt maps and explosives data records kept by a Naval base, despite decades of agency reliance on this exemption).

[67] Halstuk & Chamberlin, *supra* note 3, at 542.

[68] Dep't of State v. Washington Post Co., 456 U.S. 595 (1978).

[69] Dep't of Justice v. Reporters Committee for Freedom of the Press, 489 U.S. 749, 774 (1989) (holding that convicted criminals have a privacy interest in their rap sheets maintained by the Federal Bureau of Investigation, a federal record compiled from state and local governments that is stored by a federal agency but does not "open agency

that may also include privacy interests under Exemption 7(c) to offer additional proof that the "public interest sought to be advanced is a significant one" and that release of the information would advance that interest.[70] Such expansion of exemptions in the name of privacy over transparency has effectively undermined the purpose of FOIA as a disclosure statute. As Halstuk and Chamberlin noted:

> Congress has repeatedly reiterated the statute's strong presumption of government openness, and the Supreme Court has consistently recognized this principle for more than two decades after the FOIA's enactment. The Court's current privacy framework is the product of judicial overreaching grounded in historical revisionism that is clearly at odds with the bedrock democratic principles of accountability and transparent governance in an open society, as envisioned by FOIA's framers.[71]

It's no wonder that federal agencies feel emboldened to delay requests interminably and to deny with little fear of consequence. People seeking records in the face of hostile agencies only have recourse in federal courts, which seem to invent new reasons to deny access to records in what were intended to be narrow exemptions. Nevertheless, lawsuits under FOIA are increasing rapidly, reaching an all-time high of 498 suits filed in federal district courts in fiscal year 2015, according to tracking done by The FOIA Project, nearly double the number of lawsuits filed in fiscal year 2008.[72]

Reclaiming FOIA cannot start with the courts, which seemingly treat the act as an unnecessary intrusion upon people's privacy rather than a tool for ensuring government transparency. A new kind of law, one responsive to modern record-keeping technology and informed by half a century of failed efforts at transparency, is the only option.

Radical Transparency: Putting Openness First

Fifty years of experience have taught us that FOIA is in desperate need of an overhaul – one that goes beyond tinkering with exemptions and updating wording in the presumption of openness – if it is going to live up to its promise of providing meaningful and consistent trans-

action to the light of public scrutiny" (citing Dep't of Air Force v. Rose, 425 U.S. 352, 361 (1976)).

[70]Nat'l Archives and Records Admin. v. Favish, 541 U.S. 157, 172 (2004).

[71]Halstuk & Chamberlin, *supra* note 3, at 564.

[72]*See* David Burnham, *FOIA Lawsuits Reach Record High*, The Foia Project, Jan. 6, 2016, http://foiaproject.org/2016/01/06/foia-lawsuits-reach-record-high/ (last visited June 20, 2016).

parency. This was understandable, to some extent, in the era of paper record-keeping. In 1966, it was not plausible to require each federal agency to make thousands of boxes of paper files open for browsing at any time for any reason, particularly when those records may include material protected by important privileges or privacy laws. Similarly, in 1996, when E-FOIA was enacted, record-keeping and public access technology were not advanced beyond requiring FOIA reading rooms for commonly requested documents.

Times have changed, and the law should change, too. The 2016 amendments to FOIA may be helpful, but they are incremental adjustments for a law that continues to fail and disappoint, requiring constant repair. The Electronic Frontiers Foundation noted after Congress passed the 2016 revisions that the bill is a move in the right direction, but, "[I]t falls short of fixing some of FOIA's biggest problems, including agency delay and stonewalling."[73] Solving those problems requires a more thorough overhaul.

With Congress' intent of providing the fullest possible disclosure of federal agency records as a starting point, we propose dismantling the current FOIA and replacing it with a law guided by the following three principles:

1. Government records should be open and accessible by the public from the moment of creation, using portals and automation to reduce barriers to access as much as possible.
2. Exceptions that would result in closure or redaction should be narrow, used sparingly, determined when a record is created, and transparently reported to the public. Consequences for abusing exemptions or otherwise violating the law should be severe and swift.
3. Incentives should be shifted so that it is harder to close a record than to make it available for public inspection and copying. Government inaction should never result in delay or denial of access.

First Principle: Thinking With Portals

As the federal government moves away from paper documents and toward full electronic record-keeping and management, imagine the scenario in which a record is created by a federal agency employee, such as an email or a memo, or even a line entered into a database. The moment it is created, it automatically goes not just into the agency's

[73] Aaron Mackey, *FOIA Reform Passes In Time for 50th Anniversary*, ELECTRONIC FRONTIERS FOUNDATION, June 13, 2016, https://www.eff.org/deeplinks/2016/06/congress-passes-foia-reform-lawmakers (last visited June 20, 2016).

electronic record-keeping system, but also into a central ERKS for all federal agencies, where it is backed up and stored, and where previously existing files are updated. A bot scans the file for individually identifiable information that the government must keep private – for example, financial records, social security numbers, names of witnesses or victims in ongoing criminal investigations – and tags that document as either private as a whole or otherwise redacts the proper information. And then, the record is pushed to a central portal, freely accessible online to anyone to be searched and retrieved.

This technology, impossible half a century ago, is entirely plausible today. This is what government transparency might look like if we were to dismantle FOIA and start again with an eye on living up to the principles of "fullest possible disclosure." But we would have to shift the way we think about the law that drives record-keeping and transparency to make this happen.

When paper records were the only option, they started in the control of the agency that created and maintained them. Opening them to public inspection required a legal mandate, and, even then, the APA and the 1966 version of FOIA failed because they gave agencies too much discretion to deny, delay or otherwise limit access. From the start, the federal FOIA did not include language specifically creating a presumption of openness of government records, though courts have consistently recognized that the purpose of the law was to create "the strong presumption in favor of disclosure" by federal agencies.[74] President Obama in his 2009 Open Government Directive, called for FOIA to "be administered with a clear presumption: In the face of doubt, openness prevails."[75] Congress, in its efforts to make the presumption of openness more meaningful in 2016,[76] did not write in language to FOIA using the phrase "presumption of openness," but rather equated it to the "foreseeable harm" standard, limiting agency actions on withholding materials under exemptions only to situations in which "the agency reasonably foresees that disclosure would harm an interest protected by an exemption" or that is otherwise prohibited by law.[77]

Over time, it has become clear that this approach to the "presumption of openness" renders modern FOIA as toothless as the APA. Openness

[74]United States Dep't of State v. Ray, 502 U.S. 164, 173 (1991).

[75]Barack Obama, Memorandum for the Heads of Departments and Agencies, Subject: Freedom Of Information Act (Jan. 21, 2009).

[76]"The standard mandates that an agency may withhold information only if it *reasonably foresees a specific identifiable harm to an interest protected by an exemption, or if disclosure is prohibited by law*. This standard is commonly referred to as the 'Foreseeable Harm' standard, or the 'Presumption of Openness.'" S. Rep. 114-4 7-8, (2015).

[77]S.B. 337, 114th Cong. (2016).

on a federal agency's terms, only after it has determined whether some harm may be "reasonably foreseeable," is not openness at all. Agencies still remain the gatekeepers of records. What is needed is mandated openness from the moment a record is created – something technologically impossible in 1966, but practical today, though the use of ERKS and online portals.

Federal agencies have shown the ability to maintain online portals in many ways, such as the FOIA reading rooms mandated by E-FOIA in 1996, and court records providers such as the Public Access to Courts Electronic Records.[78] However, they have much more potential for proactive disclosures that have largely gone unfulfilled, even after President Obama's Open Government Directive calling for more proactive, online disclosures. In 2015, the FOIA Advisory Committee found that E-FOIA compliance was problematic, and it suggested that despite Department of Justice Office of Information Policy, which provided guidance for federal agencies to follow to become more proactive in posting records, "[T]here is no evidence that agencies are following it" and found only a "small increase in proactive posting government-wide."[79]

Where executive branch directives and committee recommendations have failed, legislative action can mandate and succeed. Congress can look to the states for help. In 2010, New Mexico passed a law mandating proactive online disclosure through creation of a state "sunshine portal" to serve as a "single internet web site that is free, user-friendly, searchable and accessible to the public ... to host the state's financial information for the purpose of governmental transparency and accountability to taxpayers."[80] The law mandated deadlines for creating the site and laid out materials that must be included on the site, such as operating budgets, state cash balances by account, revenue received broken down by source, state contracts of more than $20,000, appropriations for state building projects, and a list of employee positions and salaries, as well as a requirement that the site be updated "as frequently as possible but at least monthly."[81] After the site was launched in 2011, the legislature amended the law to mandate that public schools post infor-

[78]John Schwartz, *An Effort to Upgrade a Court Archive System to Free and Easy*, N.Y. Times, Feb. 12, 2009, at A16.

[79]Freedom of Information Act Federal Advisory Committee, Final Report and Recommendations 14 (Apr. 19, 2016).

[80]N.M. Stat. Ann. § 10-16D-3(A) (LexisNexis 2016).

[81]N.M. Stat. Ann. § 10-16D-3(D). The initial wording in the statute required updates to be posted to the portal "as new information is received," though that was amended. *See* S.B. 195, 49th Leg. (N.M. 2010).

mation to the Sunshine Portal as well.[82] The law called for the site to be developed through cooperation by the state's information technology, finance and administration departments, though the site was built by a private contractor for about $180,000.[83] The site has not been without its issues, including an adverse ruling by a state district judge in 2012 that required the state to remove most government employee names from the salary database,[84] but it is an example that a law mandating proactive transparency can be created and maintained in a way that is meaningful to the public.

Additionally, making federal agency records available through automation and portals would help reduce copying and processing costs, which are not insignificant. OGIS estimated that in Fiscal Year 2014, agencies "processed 647,142 FOIA requests at a cost of $462 million dollars and recouped just $4.2 million dollars from FOIA fees, less than 1 percent of the reported cost."[85]

Congress has shown a willingness to think with portals already, as the 2016 amendments call for development of a central portal for filing FOIA requests. But imagine if that central portal included access to all federal agency documents instead. The central portal would be a key for proactive disclosure of federal agency records, which FOIA overhaul supporters in Congress view as the way to "improve transparency of government operations and allow the public to better understand government activities and decisions."[86]

Second Principle: Curb Exemption Creep Through Proactive Designation

Judicial expansion of exemptions, largely in the name of protecting national security privacy, has also contributed to FOIA paralysis in federal agencies. Proactive transparency would present a challenge to the

[82] S.B. 327, 50th Leg. (N.M. 2011).

[83] *See* Tracy Dingmann, *New Portal Lets the Sun Shine on State Government*, CENTER FOR CIVIC POLICY, Dec. 17, 2010, http://civicpolicy.com/new-portal-lets-the-sun-shine-on-state-government/ (last visited June 20, 2016).

[84] Governor Susana Martinez remained committed to transparency, interpreting the court's ruling to allow her to post state employee names and salaries on a separate site outside of the Sunshine Portal, which she did. Jim Scarantino, *Gov. Martinez Relaunches Internet Access to Employee Salaries Court Ordered Removed from Sunshine Portal*, NEW MEXICO WATCHDOG, Aug. 15, 2012, http://watchdog.org/15607/nm-gov-martinez-relaunches-internet-access-to-employee-salaries-court-ordered-removed-from-sunshine-portal/ (last visited June 20, 2016).

[85] FREEDOM OF INFORMATION ACT FEDERAL ADVISORY COMMITTEE, *supra* note 79, at 10.

[86] H.R. Rep. 114-391 (2016), 11.

current FOIA system of dealing with privacy and security concerns, which, in essence, is a system where records start out closed and are only released if and when a requester can establish a right of access, as well as a sufficient reason for wanting the documents, and proof that there is likely government wrongdoing to be exposed. While this system certainly protects valid privacy and national security concerns, it also delays or denies access to far too much information that should be easily accessible by the public.

An exemption system in a proactive, transparency-first FOIA would be different. If a record starts out as open and accessible, then agency employees creating records would have to designate them as falling under a valid exemption at the start. Again, this would have been difficult if not impossible in the age of paper records, but technology makes such a system feasible. As envisioned in the previous section, the ERKS could allow a drop-down box of options to be selected by the record creator including the actual legislative exemptions – not the ones created by the judiciary – raising the employee's concerns. Names or account numbers involved that trigger privacy concerns could be redacted on the spot. If an employee intends to use an exemption, he or she could then explain the need for keeping that information out of the hands of citizens. To ensure that these exemptions were not abused, the exemptions themselves could then be made transparent, published on a daily log of exemptions on the transparency portal.

This may seem burdensome to the government employee, but as said in the tech industry, this is a feature, not a bug. Exemptions *should* be difficult and rarely used. A proactive disclosure system, with exemptions made and explained at the outset of record creation, would help address what the Senate noted in 2016 as "a growing and troubling trend towards relying on these discretionary exemptions to withhold large swaths of Government information, even though no harm would result from disclosure."[87]

It's worth remembering that identity thieves and spies don't use FOIA to cause harm, even though these are often the enemies that privacy and security point to as the reason for broader interpretation of FOIA exemptions. The information most likely to require exempting – financial accounts, Social Security records, victim and witness information in criminal investigations, identities of U.S. agents in ongoing military operations, and attorney-client communications, for example – obviously should be exempted and receive little concern from the public not being able to access them. The rest should be public, and the bur-

[87]S. Rep. 114-4 3 (2016).

den should be on government to explain why at the moment a record is created.

There would certainly be times when agency employees were unsure whether information should be redacted or exempted. In such a situation, an employee could ask the Office of Government Information Services ombuds office for guidance, either as a quick answer *via* email or conversation, or through a more formal opinion. Guidance for this kind of system can be found in Texas, where the Public Information Act requires government bodies to ask for an opinion from the attorney general's office for information that "it wishes to withhold from public disclosure and that it considers to be within one of the exceptions" under the act.[88] Decisions are to be made promptly, but no later than forty-five business days after an opinion is sought.[89] Under a proactive disclosure system, rather than waiting for a request, a government employee would seek an opinion when the issue arose, allowing a determination to be made without a requester having to wait for it.

One concern in a proactive disclosure system would be agency employees actively seeking to undermine or otherwise avoid it by using private methods of communication outside of the ERKS. This would not be a new problem; indeed, government officials appear to commonly try this tactic, including creation of a private server system in the State Department under Secretary Hillary Clinton,[90] or conducting government business on a private email account on Yahoo by former Alaska Governor Sarah Palin.[91] FOIA does not include criminal penalties within its text, though the agency may be ordered to pay "reasonable attorney fees and litigation costs" to plaintiffs who successfully sue to force compliance.[92] Employees may also face discipline for denying materials "arbitrarily or capriciously," [93] though such actions are exceedingly rare, or federal government employees may be prosecuted under the criminal code section regarding "willfully and unlawfully" concealing or destroying "any record ... filed or deposited ... in any public office."[94] A new FOIA built on principles of proactive transparency should build in criminal penalties for willful non-compliance, similar to

[88]TEXAS GOV'T CODE § 552.301(a) (LexisNexis 2016).

[89]*Id.* at § 552.306(a).

[90]*See* Steven Lee Myers & Eric Lichtblau, *State Dept. Report Faults Clinton on Email Server*, N.Y. TIMES, May 26, 2016, at A1.

[91]*See* Karl Vick, *Palin Had Another Private E-Mail Account, Company Says*, WASH. POST, Sept. 30, 2008, *available at* http://www.washingtonpost.com/wp-dyn/content/article/2008/09/30/AR2008093002699.html?tid = a_inl (last visited June 20, 2016).

[92]5 U.S.C. § 552(a)(4)(E) (2016).

[93]*Id.* at 5 U.S.C. § 552(a)(4)(F).

[94]18 U.S.C. § 2071 (2016).

state laws that build in fines and jail time as a way of deterring efforts to undermine transparency goals.[95] The OGIS should have the power to investigate and recommend sanctions for deliberate non-compliance, with referral to the Department of Justice possible for egregious cases.

Third Principle: Shift Incentives to Favor Openness

Martin Luther King Jr. once said that justice delayed is justice denied.[96] Similarly, when it comes to government transparency, often access delayed is access denied. The 2016 report on FOIA by the House of Representatives Committee on Oversight and Government Reform found, "The Biggest Barrier of All" under FOIA is "Delay, Delay, Delay."[97] While agency decisions are supposed to be made within twenty business days after receipt of a request, with an extension of up to ten days for "unusual circumstances,"[98] frequently delays are much longer, sometimes years, before agencies comply with FOIA requests.

Government inaction should not hinder the public's right to know, and yet, when the government is non-responsive to requests, the right to know suffers. The incentives built into the law favor secrecy, not transparency. It is not enough "to depend solely upon the voluntary disclosure of documents by those most likely to want to withhold them," as Nisbet, the head of OGIS, once said.[99] Currently, for the most part, a federal agency record is created in secret, it is managed and stored in secret, where it remains until a request for access – and only then if a government employee with little fear of punishment for non-compliance deems it appropriate and in his or her best interest to release after considering an array of legislatively and judicially created exemptions. The default is closure, and it takes a significant amount of work by a dogged citizen to force disclosure, and, even then, it may take a time-consuming and expensive lawsuit.

If FOIA were based in proactive transparency, it would turn this model on its head by shifting the incentives toward openness, rather than secrecy. If it were harder to apply and explain exemptions at the outset, when records are created, then the incentive would be to take the path requiring less work by just letting the record go into the ERKS

---

[95] *See* Daxton R. "Chip" Stewart, *Let the Sunshine In, or Else: An Examination of the "Teeth" of State and Federal Open Meetings and Open Records Laws*, 15 COMM. L. & POL'Y 265, 292-98 (2010).

[96] Martin Luther King Jr., *The Negro Is Your Brother*, 212 ATLANTIC MONTHLY 78, 80 (1963).

[97] FOIA IS BROKEN, *supra* note 4, at 34.

[98] 5 U.S.C. § 552(a)(6) (2016).

[99] Nisbet, *supra* note 48, at 3.

and be uploaded to the FOIA portal in the first place. Worries about under-protection of privacy may be able to be addressed through automated record-keeping bots designed to take care of some of the simpler tasks of identifying and redacting information. As the National Archives and Records Administration found in a 2014 report on automated records, "[T]ouching each file and making a separate record-keeping decision about each one" is likely to be overly burdensome for busy users, so, "automated tools for managing electronic records could reduce the recordkeeping burden on end users and lead to more consistent, scalable results, and ultimately more accessible and usable agency information."[100]

Once again, modern technology unimaginable half a century ago allows new ways of thinking about record-keeping and government openness. Building new incentives into FOIA, where the norm is transparency, where secrecy is the more difficult option, and where the record-keeping system largely automates exemptions and redaction, would enable citizens to learn about their government more effectively.

Conclusion

FOIA is irrevocably broken. It needs systemic reform, not the series of endless legislative amendments and administrative patches that have done little to actually change access law for the better in the past fifty years.

Redrafting FOIA in the digital age, *for* the digital age, is the only way to end the constant cycle of non-compliance, delay, frustration and inadequate legislative revision that has plagued the law since its initial passage. Proactive disclosure through electronic and automated record-keeping and government-hosted portals offer a chance at a culture shift to serve the underlying purpose of FOIA of full agency disclosure. Codification of proactive transparency-first FOIA system would move beyond incremental fixes at the agency and administrative level, which are improvements but nevertheless would be subject to the whim of presidential administrations and directives, to keep the emphasis on the "presumption of openness."[101]

Citizens need a technology-first solution. Government employees seek technology to help them with their jobs as well, which as the director of the Office of Information Policy Melanie Pustay said in 2015, is

[100]National Archives and Records Administration, Managing Government Records Directive: Automated Electronic Records Management Report/Plan 5 (2014).

[101]*See* S. Rep. 114-4, *supra* note 76, at 3.

"universally desired" by agencies because "any time you can replace a manual process with an electronic one, you can do things faster. It helps the processing time for individual requests, obviously, but it can also reduce staffing, which in turn can help in these fiscal times."[102]

Even critics of FOIA who see expanded transparency as potentially infringing on essential privacy norms see problems in a law that does not address technology adequately. Daniel Solove, the renowned privacy scholar, commented that in the United States, the "information regulatory infrastructure is disconnected, often outdated, and inadequate to meet the challenges of the new technologies of the Information Age."[103] An overhaul using automated records management and portals would not be intended to ignore or minimize legitimate privacy concerns, or to overturn privacy protections mandated through the Privacy Act,[104] the Family Educational Rights and Privacy Act,[105] or other essential laws requiring the government to keep certain information about individuals from being distributed to the public. Rather, a FOIA favoring proactive transparency would build in protections for privacy interests as records are created, while preventing excessive and unnecessary exemption and redaction in the name of serving those interests.

Recovering from half a century of being "Taj Mahal of Unintended Consequences" will take great public support, motivation by transparency and privacy advocates, legislative will, presidential support, and perhaps most importantly, technological design that embraces automation and public accessibility. The details and intricacies of building these portals, and getting the legislative language just right to balance the incentives and consequences, will be crucial. But these should not deter efforts to remake FOIA in a way that, at long last, would give citizens what they should expect from a transparent federal government.

[102] Anderson, *supra* note 5.

[103] Daniel J. Solove, *Access and Aggregation: Privacy, Public Records, and the Constitution*, 86 MINN. L. REV. 1137, 1152 (2002).

[104] 5 U.S.C. § 552a (2016).

[105] 20 U.S.C. §1232 et seq. (2016).

Controlling Discourse, Foreclosing Recourse: The Creep of the Glomar Response

A.Jay Wagner

The Glomar response to Freedom of Information Act requests – "we can neither confirm nor deny the existence or nonexistence of records responsive to your request" – was the product of extraordinary circumstances, to be applied sparingly by the federal government in withholding national security information. Since 2013, instances of state and local use of the Glomar response have signaled a potentially problematic expansion. Establishment of non-federal agency use of the Glomar response poses the threat of an exponential increase in the practice, making oversight difficult. This article considers the recent use of the Glomar response in four cases in which state or local agencies utilized the reply to withhold law enforcement records. The origin and case law of the Glomar response, methods for compelling disclosure after a Glomar response are considered, before a discussion of potential threats of expansion and productive paths forward.

Dr. Armando Florez was a Cuban diplomat turned dissident. He served as the chief Cuban attaché in Washington, D.C., before U.S.-Cuban relations deteriorated following the 1959 Cuban Revolution. He held prominent Cuban posts in Belgium, India and Czechoslovakia – once infamously refusing to shake the hand of the Soviet envoy.[1] He grew disillusioned with the autocratic Castro regime and, after an attempt on his partner's life, sought asylum in the United States. In exchange for intelligence on the Castro government, Florez and family were escorted by the Central Intelligence Agency from Spain to the United States. He was granted citizenship in 1979 and lived out his life working a series

---

[1]*See* C.J. Ciaramella, *The True Story of the Last Cuban Diplomat to the U.S.*, WASH. FREE BEACON, May 19, 2014, http://freebeacon.com/national-security/the-true-story-of-the-last-cuban-diplomat-to-the-u-s/.

of jobs in New York City, culminating in an editorial position with the Associated Press.[2]

As Florez slipped into early-onset Alzheimer's, his son, Sergio Florez, sought to build a record of his father's colorful, politically charged life. In doing so, he filed a 2001 Freedom of Information Act request with the CIA, hoping to get at least a sketch of his father's past. The agency agreed to release the responsive records once Sergio submitted a notarized privacy waiver signed by his father.[3] Given his father's medical condition, this was unlikely. Rather than further appeal, Sergio dropped the matter.

Shortly after his father's 2013 death, Sergio filed another FOIA request for the same information. This time, the CIA provided a different answer, utilizing the expansive powers of Exemption 1, the national security exception to disclosure, and issuing what is known as a "Glomar response" – "we can neither confirm nor deny the existence or nonexistence of records responsive to your request"[4] – despite acknowledging existence of the records in the past.[5]

Sergio Florez filed an appeal, claiming there was an inadequate search by the CIA and that use of the Glomar response was improper. Further complicating the situation, Florez had discovered two public CIA records mentioning his father.

In its decision, the United States Court of Appeals for the Second Circuit suggested the Glomar response to be appropriate so long as an "exemption itself would preclude the *acknowledgement* of such documents."[6] This burden is satisfied by submitting an affidavit to the court which bears "substantial weight" if "justifications for non-disclosure are not controverted by contrary evidence in the record or by evidence of bad faith."[7] CIA counsel declared that no matter the previously disclosed relationship, national security would be jeopardized by rejecting Florez's request in the conventional statutory manner.[8] The CIA refused the typical denial process and issued a Glomar response under the premise that recognizing any relationship between the government and the elder Florez would harm national security. The decision was

---

[2]*See* Complaint for Injunctive Relief at 6, Florez v. Central Intelligence Agency, 14-Cv-1002 (SHS), 2015 U.S. Dist. LEXIS 20009 (S.D.N.Y. Feb. 19, 2015).

[3]*See* Florez v. Cent. Intelligence Agency, 14-Cv-1002 (SHS), 2015 U.S. Dist. LEXIS 20009, *2 (S.D.N.Y. Feb. 19, 2015).

[4]Letter from Delores M. Nelson, Info. & Privacy Coordinator, CIA, to Melissa Goodman, Staff Attorney, Nat'l Sec. Project, ACLU (May 13, 2009), *available at* https://www.aclu.org/sites/default/files/pdfs/natsec/CIA_05132009.pdf.

[5]*See infra* note 23 and accompanying text.

[6]Wilner v. NSA, 592 F.3d 60, 68 (2nd Cir. 2009).

[7]*Florez*, 2015 U.S. Dist. at *7.

[8]*Id.* at *14.

affirmed even though the relationship between Armando Florez and the CIA was widely known and documented in public records.[9]

The case of the Florez family highlights a troublesome development in government implementation of the FOIA. Signed into law in 1966 by President Lyndon B. Johnson, it exists as the American public's primary method for gathering information on the activities and agents of the state.[10] The Supreme Court of the United States has reiterated this fundamental rationale for access to government records, and specifically the FOIA, as a method for holding those in power answerable to their constituency. The Court has repeatedly identified it as a crucial element to a functioning democratic government. In the 1978 case *NLRB v. Robbins Tire & Rubber Co.*, the Court stated, "The basic purpose of [the] FOIA is to ensure an informed citizenry, vital to the functioning of a democratic society, needed to check against corruption and to hold the governors accountable to the governed."[11] A decade later, the Court restated its primary function as a transparency mechanism for civilians, providing the ability to know "what their Government is up to."[12] The Court emphasized FOIA's legitimacy, suggesting it "not be dismissed as a convenient formalism. . . . It defines a structural necessity in a real democracy."[13] A 1976 opinion called for access as not only a method for educating the citizenry, but as an awl "to pierce the veil of administrative secrecy and to open agency action to the light of public scrutiny."[14] President Barack Obama[15] and the 114th Congress[16] have also recognized FOIA as a vital democratic element, affirming their commitment to an accountable and transparent government through the access statute.

[9]*Id.* at *31 ("Based on the effort shown by the CIA in its supplemental search and disclosure and the lack of contrary evidence revealing any classified interest in Dr. Florez, the CIA's Glomar response remains valid.").

[10]*See* Richard Shelby, *Accountability and Transparency: Public Access to Federally Funded Research Data*, 37 HARV. J. ON LEGIS. 369, 383 (2000) (Sen. Shelby states, "FOIA is the public's primary mechanism for accessing information held by the government.").

[11]437 U.S. 214, 242 (1978).

[12]Dep't of Justice v. Reporters Comm. for Freedom of the Press, 489 U.S. 749, 773 (1989).

[13]Nat'l Archives and Records Admin. v. Favish, 541 U.S. 157, 171-72 (2004).

[14]Dep't of Air Force v. Rose, 425 U.S. 352, 361 (1976).

[15]Presidential Memorandum for Heads of Executive Departments and Agencies Concerning the Freedom of Information Act, 74 Fed. Reg. 4683, 4683 (Jan. 21, 2009) ("In our democracy, the Freedom of Information Act. . . is the most prominent expression of a profound national commitment to ensuring an open Government.").

[16]S. REP. NO. 114-4, at 2 (2015) (The Freedom of Information Act "has become an indispensable tool for ensuring our Government remains transparent and accountable to the people.").

Scholars have conducted significant research on the purpose of FOIA, with a consensus that access statutes ultimately must help generate an informed public.[17] The prevailing notion is that without access to government information, we cannot understand "the paradoxical relation between free men and their legislative agents."[18] In an early study on the FOIA and the necessity of an informed public, Lillian BeVier pointed to the guiding voice of such thought: "The conception of democracy apparently embraced by proponents of the 'right to know' echoes the view of Alexander Meiklejohn, whose insights into the relevance of self-government to First Amendment analysis have been of seminal importance."[19]

Yet, fulfilling this covenant between the public and its elected officials has proven difficult, fraught with concerns of government malfeasance and disingenuousness in implementing the FOIA.[20] The Glomar response presents a specific set of issues, most notably (1) a curtailment of the appeals process, and as a result, (2) a destabilizing of the primary purpose of the access statute: providing the material for an informed public able to knowledgeably participate in a robust public discourse.

The Glomar response was created as an unusual tactic to be applied in only extraordinary circumstances. In legally short-circuiting the FOIA mechanism, it accords with a diplomatic imperative – protecting national security. But recently, the Glomar response has seen expanded application, finding use not only across the exemption spectrum but also cascading into state FOIA replies. State-level courts have for the first time begun considering the Glomar response's place in non-federal

[17] *See* SHANNON E. MARTIN, FREEDOM OF INFORMATION: THE NEWS MEDIA USE (2008); Fred H. Cate, D. Annette Fields & James K. McBain, *The Right to Privacy and the Public's Right to Know: The "Central Purpose" of the Freedom of Information Act*, 46 ADMIN. L. REV. 41 (1994); Phillip J. Cooper, *The Supreme Court, the First Amendment, and Freedom of Information,* 46 PUB. ADMIN. REV. 622 (1986); Thomas I. Emerson, *Legal Foundations of the Right to Know*, 1976 WASH. U. L. Q. 1 (1976); Martin E. Halstuk, *Blurred Vision: How Supreme Court FOIA Opinions on Invasion of Privacy Have Missed the Target of Legislative Intent*, 4 COMM. L. & POL'Y 111 (1999).

[18] Alexander Meiklejohn, *The First Amendment Is an Absolute*, 1961 SUP. CT. REV. 245, 255.

[19] Lillian R. BeVier, *An Informed Public, an Informing Press: The Search for a Constitutional Principle*, 68 CAL. L. REV 483, 503 (1980).

[20] *See Ensuring Agency Compliance with the Freedom of Information Act, Hearing Before Comm. on Oversight & Gov't. Reform*, 114th Cong. (2015); *Ensuring Government Transparency Through FOIA Reform: Hearing Before Subcomm. on Gov't. Op.*, 114th Cong. (2015); REPORT OF THE COMMISSION ON PROTECTING AND REDUCING GOVERNMENT SECRECY, S. DOC. NO. 105-2 (1997); Steven Aftergood, *Reducing Government Secrecy: Finding What Works*, 27 YALE L. & POL. REV. 399 (2009); David E. Pozen, *The Mosaic Theory, National Security, and the Freedom of Information Act*, 115 YALE L. J. 628 (2005); Josh Gerstein, *Judge Says Hillary Clinton's Private Emails Violated Policy*, POLITICO, Aug. 20, 2015, http://www.politico.com/story/2015/08/judge-says-hillary-clintons-private-emails-violated-policy-121568.

access statutes, portending a possible explosion of implementation.[21] Federal use of the Glomar response has faced considerable scrutiny in the courtroom, the press[22] and among transparency advocates and scholars,[23] but state and local claims pose the possibility of limited oversight. In less populous jurisdictions, with fewer interested individuals and less familiarity with the intricacies of access statutes, the risk of exploitation rises.

Outside of litigation and anecdotal reports, use of the non-disclosure rationale is difficult to track as it exists predominately as a common law mechanism, and no formal efforts in accounting for its implementation have ever been established. Since the 1976 case *Phillippi*

[21] Brief for Reporters Comm. for Freedom of the Press as Amicus Curiae, p. 15, Abdur-Rashid v. N.Y. City Police Dep't, 992 N.Y.S. 2d 870 (2014) ("Permitting the NYPD and other agencies to issue Glomar-like responses to FOIA requests is likely to only intensify what is a growing and problematic trend toward secrecy at all levels of government.").

[22] *See* Brian Anderson, *Glomar: The Ship that Sinks FOIA Requests*, VICE, June 20, 2012, *available at* http://motherboard.vice.com/blog/glomar; Jameel Jaffer & Nathan Freed Wessler, *The C.I.A.'s Misuse of Secrecy*, N.Y. TIMES, Apr. 30, 2012, *available at* http://www.nytimes.com/2012/04/30/opinion/the-cias-misuse-of-secrecy.html?_r=0; Karen McVeigh, *Drone Strikes: Activists Seek to Life Lid on Open Secret of Targeted Killings*, THE GUARDIAN, June 20, 2012 *available at* http://www.theguardian.com/world/2012/jun/20/drone-strikes-targeted-killings-case?intcmp=239; Kevin Collier, *NSA Emails Show How Much Work the Agency Does to Say Nothing*, THE DAILY DOT, June 28, 2014, http://www.dailydot.com/politics/nsa-foia-glomar-response-emails/; Jeff Larson, *NSA: Responding to this FOIA Would Help "Our Adversaries,"* PROPUBLICA, June 25, 2013, https://www.propublica.org/article/nsa-responding-to-this-foia-would-help-our-adversaries; David Kravets, *CIA Must End Silence on Drone Targeted Kills*, WIRED, Mar. 15, 2013, http://www.wired.com/2013/03/cia-drones-foia/.

[23] *See* Michael D. Becker, *Piercing Glomar: Using the Freedom of Information Act and the Official Acknowledgement Doctrine to Keep Government Secrecy in Check*, 62, ADMIN. L. REV. 673, 700 (2012) (calling the Glomar response important, but advocating a lower official acknowledgement threshold.); Gregory G. Brooker, *FOIA Exemption 3 and the CIA: An Approach to End the Confusion and Controversy*, 68 MINN. L. REV., 1231, 1261 (1984) (suggesting FOIA amendments less deferential to national security claims akin to Glomar responses.); Joshua R. Chazen, *Electronic Privacy Information Center v. National Security Agency: How Glomar Responses Benefit Businesses and Provide an Epic Blow to Individuals*, 9 J. BUS. & TECH. L. 315, 334 (2014) (arguing that in the titular case the D.C. Circuit skewed FOIA law towards business interests by recognizing the Glomar response due to vague cyber security concerns.); Andrew Christy, *The ACLU's Hollow FOIA Victory Over Drone Strikes*, 21 GEO. MASON L. REV. 1, 15 (2013) (lamenting the ACLU victory as effectively useless as "the threshold [for official acknowledgement] is still too high to be useful in other cases."); John Y. Gotanda, *Glomar Denials under FOIA: A Problematic Privilege and a Proposed Alternative Procedure of Review*, 56 U. PITT. L. REV. 165, 183-85 (1994) (suggesting the lack of judicial scrutiny of Glomar response is disputable, offering a new "credible evidence" review standard for Glomar claims.); Amy E. Rees, *Recent Developments Regarding the Freedom of Information Act: A "Prologue to a Farce or a Tragedy; or, Perhaps Both,"* 44 DUKE L.J. 1183, 1190 (1994-95) ("[A]pplication of [the Glomar response] has in recent cases become unsatisfactory. The procedural requirements are being used as a substitute for courts' judgments on the merits.").

v. CIA,[24] in which the D.C. Circuit first considered the legitimacy of the term, according to Lexis Nexis's comprehensive legal database, the case has been cited in 287 federal FOIA decisions.[25] The 1981 case *Military Audit Project v. Casey*,[26] where the court recognized the Glomar response as an appropriate reply, has been cited in 951 federal cases.

Until 2013, neither *Phillippi* nor *Military Audit Project* was mentioned in a published state court opinion. Since then, state courts in New York and the District of Columbia have considered three cases where either *Phillippi*, *Military Audit Project* or both were cited after local law enforcement provided Glomar responses to state records requests.[27] A Lexis-Nexis search uncovered an Illinois case related to the "Glomar response,"[28] and a search of the same phrase in the Google Scholar case law search turned up a decision involving the New York City Police Department.[29] A 2013 New Jersey case considers the legality of the "confirm nor deny the existence" language without citing federal Glomar cases or using the "Glomar response" phrase. Of these six responsive cases, two are ultimately unrelated to the specific cause of the Glomar response,[30] leaving four state-level cases - *North Jersey Media Group v. Bergen County Prosecutor's Office*,[31] *Better Government Association v. Zaruba*,[32] *Abdur-Rashid v. New York City Police Department*,[33] and *Hashmi v. New York City Police Department*[34] considering

[24]546 F.2d 1009, 1013 (D.C. Cir. 1976).

[25]Lexis-Nexis was searched for cases in which the Glomar response was used. There is no other formal documentation of the practice and for the purposes of this study, the search of the Lexis Nexis case database represents as consistent of an accounting measure available.

[26]656 F.2d 724 (D.C. Cir. 1981).

[27]One of which, *Fraternal Order of Police v. District of Columbia*, 79 A.3d 347, 356 (D.C. 2013), referenced *Military Audit Project* in considering the "bad faith" standard and is unrelated to concerns related to the Glomar response.

[28]In an effort to capture all relevant cases regarding the Glomar response, a second search of the Lexis Nexis database was conducted. The second query used the search phrase "Glomar response." For the purposes of this study, in review of all Lexis Nexis results, cases unrelated to the FOIA were removed from consideration.

[29]The Google Scholar case database was also queried for landmark cases and key search phrases to ensure all relevant cases were included in the study.

[30]The two were *Asian American Fund v. New York City Police Department*, 41 Misc. 3d 471 (N.Y.S. 2013), which made no explicit reference to any Glomar-related issues and is primarily concerned with investigatory exemptions; and *Fraternal Order of Police*, 79 A.3d 347 (D.C. 2013); *see also supra* note 27.

[31]No. BER-L-6741-13 LEXIS 2766 (N.J. Super. Ct. L. Div. Nov. 15, 2013).

[32]21 N.E.3d 516 (Ill. App. 2d 2014).

[33]992 N.Y.S. 2d 870 (2014).

[34]998 N.Y.S.2d 596 (2014).

the applicability of the Glomar response in non-federal claims. In addition to these court decisions, Indiana amended language to its state access statute, the Access to Public Records Act, in 2013 that effectively codified the Glomar response.[35]

Legal recognition on the state level threatens freedom of information laws at their most basic, grassroots level, making them liable to a precipitous rise in the number of Glomar responses, impugning the very integrity of access and transparency laws. This rash of like cases, along with the statutory amendment, signals the possibility of new paradigm in access law, one where equivocation passes as an acceptable and common reply. Acquiring sensitive information is difficult enough under current regimes. Adding a layer of ambiguity, appropriate only when dealing with the most precarious of records and information, is a bridge too far. It would provide a power originally crafted for the protection of national security secrets to rank-and-file police forces in towns and villages across the country.

This study seeks to document the early evidence of the Glomar response moving into state and local FOI laws. It will do so by exploring the origins of the Glomar response as a result of the heightened political tensions of the Cold War, before considering several recent decisions in New York, Illinois and New Jersey, where courts considered cases of state and local authorities denying access to records with Glomar response claims. These cases mark a new territory for the practice, which originally saw use as a federal response to national security threats. The four decisions discussed herein demonstrate this expanded use; each involves local police authorities refusing a records request with a Glomar response justified by law enforcement exemption claim. Coincidentally, all of the denied requests were seeking information that would have provided oversight of the law enforcement agency, and each received a Glomar response where previously such a request would have been available or withheld according to conventional FOIA procedure.

The next section documents the disconcerting nature of the Glomar response as the official acknowledgement and waiver of exemption protection standards for appealing such a reply have proved particularly challenging to overcome. The article concludes with recent legislative efforts to constrain use of the Glomar response and a discussion of the threat and potential ways forward.

[35] IND. CODE ANN. §§ 5-14-3-4.4 (Pub. L. 248-2013 § 4) (2013) (allowing for information appropriate to the state's investigatory or criminal intelligence exemptions to fall into a Glomar response.).

THE FOUNDATIONS OF THE GLOMAR RESPONSE

The Glomar response originates in an unusual Cold War story, in which a sunken Soviet submarine lay on the Pacific floor. Interested in the possibility of nuclear weapons, codebooks and cryptographic machines, the CIA launched Project Azorian to retrieve the sub from three miles underwater.[36] The complicated effort would draw public attention, and, in an attempt to keep the project clandestine, the CIA brought on board eccentric millionaire Howard Hughes, developing a cover story that Hughes was searching the deep for the valuable mineral manganese.[37] The name of the ship was the Hughes Global Marine Explorer, with "Glomar" the portmanteau of "Global Marine."[38]

Shortly after publication of the Pentagon Papers and the Watergate scandal, government skepticism was high and the FOIA was newly strengthened by a 1974 amendment.[39] The CIA received a torrent of FOIA requests for information on its curious efforts.[40] Hoping to keep the Soviets unaware of the project and protect a considerable expenditure in resources (and the ultimate failure of the project), the associate general counsel at the CIA was charged with crafting a FOIA response allowing the organization to retain its secrets, without lying.[41] The result is the Glomar response – "we can neither confirm nor deny the existence of requested records" – that allows agencies to make an end-run around the FOIA.

The Glomar language, established under these very unusual circumstances where national security and diplomatic concerns were at stake, soon found traction in a wider range of non-disclosure claims. National security concerns became conflated with internal disciplinary reports, individuals' law enforcement files and the government's relationship with Google. The related federal case history demonstrates the Glomar response distancing itself from its original purpose, moving from a rare exception to regular application. The proliferation occurred under little oversight and for much of its life with no government guidance or

[36] *See* DAVID H. SHARP, THE CIA'S GREATEST COVER OPERATION: INSIDE THE DARING MISSION TO RECOVER A NUCLEAR-ARMED SOVIET SUB (2012).

[37] *See Radiolab: Neither Confirm Nor Deny*, WNYC, Feb. 12, 2014, *available at* http://www.radiolab.org/story/confirm-nor-deny/.

[38] *See id.*

[39] Privacy Act, Pub. L. 93-502, 88 Stat. 1561-1564; §§ 1-3 (1974).

[40] *Radiolab, supra* note 37.

[41] *See* Nate Jones, *"Neither Confirm, Nor Deny": The History of the Glomar Response*, NAT. SEC. ARCHIVES, Feb. 11, 2014, *available at* https://nsarchive.word-press.com/2014/02/11/neither-confirm-nor-deny-the-history-of-the-glomar-response-and-the-glomar-explorer/.

regulation. The Glomar response did, however, find pushback from the public, facing frequent challenges in the courtroom, including two appeals on the inaugural application.[42]

Phillippi v. CIA

Reticence from federal judges was evident in the early cases considering use of the Glomar response. The Glomar Explorer operation was splashed onto the front page of the *New York Times* in a Seymour Hersh story.[43] Reporter Harriet Ann Phillippi, among others, followed up and filed a FOIA request with the CIA seeking information on the covert mission. The CIA supplied her with the original Glomar response, which she challenged in federal court. In an initial appeal, the D.C. Circuit determined that the evasive reply did not comply with previous Exemption 1 decisions requiring an affidavit justifying nondisclosure.[44] In fact, the ambiguity curtailed scrutiny of any kind, be it *in camera* or a written justification subject to "criticism and illumination by a party with the actual interest in forcing disclosure."[45] The case was remanded due to a technicality.[46] On the second appeal, the new Jimmy Carter administration dropped the Glomar response language from the denial, and the D.C. Circuit ruled that records on the Glomar Explorer operation were properly withheld according to Exemptions 1 and 3, the national security and other statutes exemptions.[47]

Military Audit Project v. Casey

The 1981 *Philllippi* decision rested on the "strikingly similar"[48] case of *Military Audit Project v. Casey*,[49] where an organization sought similar records regarding the Glomar Explorer. This time, the Glomar language remained in the appeal, and the court was faced with confronting the legality of the "neither confirm nor deny" response. In considering

[42]*See* Military Audit Project v. Casey, 656 F.2d 724 (D.C. Cir. 1981); Phillippi v. CIA, 546 F.2d 1009 (D.C. Cir. 1976).

[43]Seymour Hersh, *CIA Salvage Ship Brought Up Part of Soviet Sub Lost in 1968*, N.Y. TIMES, Mar. 19, 1975, *available at* http://www.nytimes.com/1975/03/19/archives/cia-salvage-ship-brought-up-part-of-soviet-sub-lost-1968-failed-to.html?_r=0

[44]*Phillippi*, 546 F.2d at 1013.

[45]*Id.* (quoting Vaughn v. Rosen, 484 F.2d 820, 825 (1973)).

[46]*Id.* at 1015.

[47]Phillippi v. CIA, 655 F.2d 1325, 1333 (D.C. Cir. 1981).

[48]*Id.* at 1328.

[49]656 F.2d 724 (D.C. Cir. 1981).

the Exemption 1 claim, the court isolated the question as to whether the documents "reasonably could be expected to cause serious damage to the national security," the standard established in President Carter's national security order.[50] The decision included a category-by-category analysis of the varying information under consideration, before deciding whether Exemption 1 was satisfied, allowing summary judgment. In deliberating whether the Glomar response fulfilled the FOIA obligation, the court, with little elaboration, accepted use of the method as in line with the tenets of the FOIA and national security protections, comparing the Glomar response outcome as comparable to a conventional summary judgement under an exemption claim.[51]

Hunt v. CI

In the 1992 case of a prisoner seeking records to exonerate himself, the Ninth Circuit ruled on a Glomar response of a request by an accused murderer seeking CIA information on the murdered individual.[52] Danae Aitchison called the case a test of whether an "agency's claimed exemptions fit the records, or if they are a mere pretext for withholding information."[53] The appellant, Joe Hunt, who was on trial in California for the murder of an Iranian national, requested information on the victim and, specifically, on the victim's relationship with the CIA.[54] Hunt appealed the Glomar response, questioning whether affidavits allowed for summary judgment under FOIA Exemptions 1 and 3. The decision confirmed that President Ronald Reagan's executive order allowed for an agency to "refuse to confirm or deny the existence or nonexistence of requested information whenever the fact of its existence or non-existence is itself classifiable under the Order."[55] In ruling that the records were appropriately classified, the Ninth Circuit registered wariness in the latitude and discretion given to national security agencies like the CIA in Glomar responses.[56] The court held, "Nevertheless, nothing in the statute or case precedent permits us to reach a different

[50]Exec. Order 12065, 43 Fed. Reg. 28949 § 3-505 (June 28, 1978).

[51]656 F.2d at 749.

[52]Hunt v. CIA, 981 F.2d 1116 (9th Cir. 1992).

[53]Danae J. Aitchison, *Reining in the Glomar Response: Reducing CIA Abuse of the Freedom of Information Act*, 27 U.C. DAVIS L. REV. 219, 243 (1993).

[54]981 F.2d at 1117.

[55]Exec. Order No. 12356, 47 Fed. Reg.14874 at 174 (Apr. 2, 1982).

[56]981 F.2d at 1120 ("[W]ith this decision, we are now 'only a short step [from] exempting all CIA records' from FOIA. That result may well be contrary to what Congress intended.").

result,"[57] before acknowledging that were this issue to be addressed it was the legislature's duty to do so.[58]

Smith v. FBI

In 2009, a federal court considered a Glomar response claim as part of a larger FOIA appeal, where the requester sought the disciplinary records of an FBI agent. In protecting the agent's privacy, with a special mention of Exemption 6, the personal privacy exemption,[59] the FBI provided a Glomar response.[60] In affirming use of the response, the District of Columbia federal district court determined that the requester had failed to show an overriding public interest in the records and confirmation of "adverse action or disciplinary reports ... would necessarily reveal precise information Exemption 6 shields."[61] The decision effectively removed many of the FBI's internal punishment documents from the ambit of not only public scrutiny but from FOIA consideration altogether, as the D.C. District Court accepted that the mere acknowledgement of a disciplinary record was an invasion of individual privacy.

Wolf v. CIA

In a pivotal 2007 decision, the D.C. Circuit ruled on a requester's ability to compel agency disclosure after receiving a Glomar response. The case involved historian Paul Wolf and his efforts to receive the CIA records of an assassinated Colombian politician.[62] Most noteworthy, Wolf contested that the CIA had waived its right to issue a Glomar response when then-CIA Director Roscoe Hillenkoetter read from CIA files at a 1948 congressional hearing, making direct reference to the Colombian politician Jorge Eliecer Gaitan. In recognizing "official acknowledgement," the court stated, "In most waiver cases, the inquiry turns on the match between the information requested and the content of the prior disclosure."[63] This proposal, matching the "specific

---

[57] *Id.*

[58] *Id.*

[59] 5 U.S.C. § 552(b)(2) (2012) (Exemption 6 excludes "personnel and medical files and similar files the disclosure of which would constitute a clearly unwarranted invasion of personal privacy.")

[60] Smith v. FBI, 663 F. Supp. 2d 1, 4 (D.D.C. 2009).

[61] *Id.*

[62] Wolf v. CIA, 473 F.3d 370 (D.C. Cir. 2007).

[63] *Id.* at 378.

information at issue"[64] with what has been publicized, becomes particularly difficult for the requester when the very existence of the sought records is in question. The court determined that the CIA director's public discussion of the Colombian politician disqualified the CIA from making a Glomar response claim on records involving Gaitan. The case was remanded so that the lower court could consider whether the records previously given a Glomar response were appropriately withheld according to statutory exemptions. The district court ruled all newly acknowledged records were aptly withheld according to Exemptions 1 and 3.[65]

Electronic Privacy Information Center v. NSA

After a 2010 cyberattack on Google, the company altered its privacy and encryption methods. As a result, the Electronic Privacy Information Center filed a FOIA request seeking communications between the NSA and Google. The NSA issued a Glomar response tethered to Exemption 3 (in particular, Section 6 of the National Security Act).[66] The court decided against EPIC, ruling the Glomar response appropriate in "excers[ing] caution when the information requested 'implicat[es] national security, a uniquely executive purview.'"[67] EPIC argued that a public relationship existed between Google and the NSA, and, thus, a Glomar response was inappropriate. The D.C. Circuit agreed that a public relationship existed, but ruled that this public relationship accounted for NSA activity, qualifying for nondisclosure under Section 6 of the NSA Act. This creates a double-bind between intelligence organizations that hold "operational files" exemptions[68] and requesters' ability to appeal Glomar responses. Nonetheless, the D.C. Circuit ruled that not only is the operational files provision adequate in Glomar response claims, but that the provision would receive a generous interpretation in federal courts, finding it "broadly exempts any information pertaining to the agency's 'activities' or 'functions.'"[69]

[64] Pub. Citizen v. Dep't of State, 11 F.3d 198, 202 (D.C. Cir.1993).

[65] Wolf v. CIA, 569 F. Supp. 2d 1 (D.D.C. 2008).

[66] Elec. Privacy Info. Ctr. v. NSA, 678 F.3d 926 (D.C. Cir. 2012) (citing Section 6 of the National Secrecy Act, 50 U.S.C. § 3144 (2006)).

[67] *Id.* at 930 (quoting Ctr. for Nat'l Sec. Studies v. Dep't of Justice, 331 F.3d 918, 926-27 (D.C. Cir. 2003)).

[68] In addition to the NSA, these agencies hold "operational files" exemptions: the CIA (50 U.S.C. § 3141) (1984), the National Geospatial-Intelligence Agency (50 U.S.C. § 3142) (1999), and the National Reconnaissance Office (50 U.S.C. § 3143) (2002).

[69] 678 F.3d at 933.

The legal berth shown to the Glomar response directly relates to the lack of judicial scrutiny in national security exemption cases. The *EPIC* and *Hunt* opinions demonstrate the *laissez faire* attitude common to courts' opinions to the national security exemption. While the FOIA statute itself has been amended and judicial doctrine has evolved, Justice Potter Stewart's concurring opinion in 1974's *EPA v. Mink* best exemplifies judicial deference to the national security exemption in FOIA cases: "(I)n enacting Section 552(b) (1) Congress chose, instead, to decree blind acceptance of executive fiat."[70] "Executive fiat" refers to the prevailing national security executive order, a decree released by all presidents since Harry Truman, save Gerald Ford and George H.W. Bush, outlining their specific visions of national security interests. For a records refusal based on Exemption 1 to be upheld, it merely must meet this shifting standard. As the development of the Glomar response and judicial interpretation of the reply are inextricably tied with the national security exemption, it follows that the Glomar response has met a similarly deferential fate in the courts. In matters of national security, courts have determined that deference to national security experts to be the preferred path.[71]

A Recent Evolution in the Glomar Response

As previously indicated, the Glomar response was born of an uncommon situation. It was established in an effort to protect critical national security information, and, as a result, evolved in tandem with Exemption 1, an exemption that has received an especially broad interpretation in adjudication. In his national security executive order, President George W. Bush explicitly established it as an appropriate federal agency reply to FOIA requests of records seen to have national security implications.[72] The Glomar response cannot be invoked independently, however. The Second Circuit ruled that "an agency must 'tether' its refusal to respond… to one of the nine FOIA exemptions."[73] The combination of national security origins and requisite connection to an exemption has manifested itself in a tight correlation of Exemptions 1 and 3 with the Glomar response.

[70] 410 U.S. 73, 95 (1973).

[71] *See, e.g.,* Larson v. Dep't of State, 565 F.3d 857, 865 (D.C. Cir. 2009) ("Today we reaffirm our deferential posture in FOIA cases regarding the 'uniquely executive purview' of national security."). *See also* Pub. Citizen v. Dep't of State, 11 F.3d 198 (D.C. Cir. 1993); Pub. Citizen v. Dep't of State, 276 F.3d 634 (D.C. Cir. 2002).

[72] Exec. Order No. 12,958, as amended, § 3.6(a), 68 Fed. Reg. 15,315 (Mar. 28, 2003).

[73] Wilner v. NSA, 592 F.3d 60, 68 (2nd Cir. 2009).

In recent years, the Glomar response has encountered expanded use, broadening in two directions: horizontally across the exemption spectrum and vertically into state and local use. Law enforcement exemptions are customary in access to records statutes, and due to overlap between policing efforts and national security concern this has resulted in Glomar responses tied to law enforcement and investigatory exemptions. *Smith* provided an example of a Glomar response under the rationale of privacy, utilizing Exemptions 6 and 7(C), a subexemption of the law enforcement exemption.[74] Another recent request saw a Glomar response pegged to Exemption 2.[75]

In October 2014, *New York Times* journalist Ron Nixon published a story on United States Postal Service's surveillance of individual mail.[76] The expose detailed the "mail covers" program, where, in targeted instances, the USPS tracks the names and addresses on the mail of individuals. Nixon cited records from a series of FOIA requests as his primary source of information, even writing a complementary blog post on the FOIA process itself.[77]

Following up on the story, another media outlet submitted a FOIA request seeking the same records.[78] In reply, the USPS issued a Glomar response under Exemption 2 ("related solely to the internal personnel rules and practices of an agency"[79]), though Nixon had published two stories explicating the records, uploaded thirty-five pages of the documents online,[80] and appeared on the *PBS NewsHour* to discuss the mail covers program.[81]

[74] 5 U.S.C. § 552(b)(7)(C) (2012).

[75] 5 U.S.C. § 552(b)(2) (2012).

[76] Ron Nixon, *Report Reveals Wider Tracking of Mail in U.S.*, N.Y. TIMES, Oct. 27, 2014, *available at* http://www.nytimes.com/2014/10/28/us/ussecretly-monitoring-mail-of-thousands.html?_r=0&module=ArrowsNav&contentCollection=U.S.&action=keypress&region=FixedLeft&pgtype=article.

[77] Ron Nixon, *Tracking the Postal Surveillance System*, N.Y. TIMES, Oct. 28, 2014, *available at* http://www.nytimes.com/times-insider/2014/10/28/tracking-the-postal-surveillance-system/.

[78] Alex Richardson & Joshua Eaton, *Postal Service and the IRS Join CIA in Handing Out Glomar Denial*, MUCKROCK, Mar. 17, 2015, https://www.muckrock.com/news/archives/2015/mar/17/postal-service-and-irs-join-cia-handing-out-glomar/.

[79] 5 U.S.C. § 552(b)(2) (2012).

[80] Ron Nixon, *Mail Covers: Snail Mail Surveillance*, N.Y. TIMES, July 3, 2013, *available at* http://www.nytimes.com/interactive/2013/06/30/us/30postal-mail-cover-documents.html?_r=0.

[81] *See How the Postal Service Is Helping Law Enforcement Monitor Snail Mail*, PBS NEWSHOUR, Oct. 28, 2014, http://www.pbs.org/newshour/bb/postal-service-helping-law-enforcement-monitor-snail-mail/.

Another recent FOIA request received a Glomar response, invoking no less than four qualifying exemptions.[82] In seeking information on IRS whistleblowers, the Department of Treasury could neither confirm nor deny the existence of the records due to a possible "unwanted invasion of personal privacy,"[83] the law enforcement privacy provision,[84] fear of disclosing a confidential source of law enforcement[85] and as statutorily exempted[86] by Internal Revenue Code.[87]

Perhaps more disconcerting is the vertical progression of the Glomar response with states looking to utilize the technique. While national security concerns have salience at various levels of governance, allowing the latitude of the Glomar response on state and local levels threatens access to an incredible amount of government records, especially considering the deference that comes part and parcel with the Glomar response. Yet, since 2012, four state courts have considered the legitimacy of the practice in application to state freedom of information laws. The four cases center on law enforcement agencies using the Glomar response to withhold records traditionally exempted according to the statutory procedure.

New Jersey Media Group v. Bergen County Prosecutor's Office

In 2013, a New Jersey reporter submitted a request through the state's Open Records Act[88] for law enforcement reports, complaints, 911 calls and communications regarding a local pastor alleged to have been involved in sexual misconduct. The Bergen County Prosecutor's Office replied, declining to indicate "whether it possesses any records that are responsive."[89] The North Jersey Media Group filed an appeal, and a trial court declined to compel disclosure, determining, "[T]he investigation of an individual that has not been arrested nor charged with a

[82]Leonard v. Dep't of Treasury, No. 10-6625, 2012 WL 813837 (D.N.J. Mar. 9, 2012).

[83]5 U.S.C. § 552(b)(6) (2012).

[84]5 U.S.C. § 552(b)(7)(c) (2012).

[85]5 U.S.C. § 552(b)(7)(d) (2012).

[86]5 U.S.C. § 552(b)(3) (2012).

[87]6103(a) & 6103(e)(7) (2012).

[88]N.J.S.A. 47:1A-1 et seq. (2001) ("[G]overnment records shall be accessible for inspection, copying, or examination by the citizens of this state, with certain exceptions, for the protection of the public interest, and any limitations on the right of access ...shall be construed in favor of the public's right to access.").

[89]North Jersey Media Group v. Bergen County Prosecutor's Office, No. BER-L-6741-13 LEXIS 2766, *2 (N.J. Super. Ct. L. Div. Nov. 15, 2013).

crime generally must not be disclosed as privacy concerns outweigh the public's need for information."[90] The Media Group appealed to the state superior court, claiming the lower court had "created a new exemption,"[91] with the court ultimately ruling in favor of non-disclosure.

Finding "in favor of accepting the defendants' reasonable expectation of privacy," the court has effectively moved a huge swath of public records outside the domain of the New Jersey access to records law.[92] Acknowledgement and appropriate exemption of private information does not imply innocence or guilt, but in allowing a Glomar response, New Jersey courts have undercut the stated objections of the OPRA and access laws generally.

Abdur-Rashid v. New York City Police Department

In a case involving a New York City-based Imam and his attempts to discover whether he or his congregation was being surveilled, Talib W. Abdur-Rashid, head of the Mosque of Islamic Brotherhood, submitted a records request *via* New York State's open records law,[93] suspecting that the New York Police Department had been surreptitiously watching the activities of his mosque.[94] His request was denied, using Glomar language, "neither confirm nor deny."[95] The Reporters Committee for Freedom of the Press has suggested the effort to be first known state-level case considering the federally established Glomar response doctrine.[96] The opinion directly addressed transferring the federally recognized Glomar response to New York State's freedom of information law, finding that existing precedent "has explicitly stated that it is beyond question that FOIA applies only to federal and not to state agencies."[97] Nevertheless, the court ruled against Abdur-Rashid and allowed the Glomar response, having found the state's appeal for confidentiality in ongoing law enforcement investigations and the safety of police informants particularly persuasive.[98]

[90] *Id.* at *35.
[91] *Id.* at *23.
[92] *Id.* at *43.
[93] N.Y. State Freedom of Information Law, Pub. Off. L. art. 6 § 84 et seq. (2014).
[94] Abdur-Rashid v. N.Y. City Police Dep't, 992 N.Y.S. 2d 870, 873 (2014).
[95] *Id.*
[96] Adam Marshall, *Glomar Surfaces in State Courts*, Reporters Committee for Freedom of the Press (2015), http://www.rcfp.org/browse-media-law-resources/news-media-law/news-media-and-law-winter-2015/glomar-surfaces-state-court.
[97] *Abdur-Rashid,* 992 N.Y.S. 2d at 894.
[98] *Id.* at 895.

Hashmi v. New York City Police Department

The Supreme Court of New York heard a similar case a few months later.[99] After reading a series of Associated Press stories on NYPD surveillance of Muslims, Samir Hashmi, treasurer of the Rutgers University Muslim Student Association, submitted a FOIL request seeking records on possible surveillance of himself and his organization. In reply, the NYPD issued a Glomar response, explaining, "[M]ere disclosure of the existence of such documents would 'cause substantial harm to the integrity and efficacy of NYPD's investigations.'"[100]

The NYPD had implored the court to adopt the Glomar response, "as a common law amendment to a statutory scheme."[101] The court ruled in favor of Hashmi, ordering the NYPD to issue a full response to the original request. The court also issued a strong rebuke on state-level Glomar use:

> The insertion of the Glomar doctrine into FOIL would build an impregnable wall against disclosure of any information concerning the NYPD's anti-terrorism activities. The wall would be created by the procedures used to vet a Glomar response, outlined above, which ensure that the decision to approve or deny a Glomar response is made with very little information, and with almost no useful input from the person or entity seeking the documents. A Glomar response virtually stifles an adversary proceeding.[102]

Over a period of three months, different districts of the New York Supreme Court came to different conclusions on use of the Glomar response. The *Hashmi* court directly addressed establishing the practice in the state's FOIL, finding the Glomar response to upset the balance between accountability and secrecy.[103]

Better Government Association v. Zaruba

In another case considering oversight of law enforcement, an investigative non-profit based in Chicago requested records from DuPage County on the activities of Patrick Zaruba, the son of DuPage County

[99] Hashmi v. N.Y. City Police Dep't, 998 N.Y.S.2d 596 (2014).
[100] *Id.* at 597.
[101] *Id.* at 722.
[102] *Id.* at 722-23.
[103] *Id.* at 724.

Sheriff John Zaruba.[104] Acting on a tip that the high school-aged Zaruba had been acting in the capacity of a law enforcement agent, the Better Government Association sought records demonstrating police activities on the younger Zaruba's part, including access to electronic databases.[105] In particular, BGA was interested in discovering whom Patrick Zaruba was searching for in the criminal databases. The Illinois Appellate Court issued an opinion extensively citing a federal court ruling on a Glomar response claim, where a records request from similar criminal repository in Texas was determined to be appropriate due to the risk of circumvention presented by allowing citizens to query the database.[106] In approving the Glomar response, the court stated, "[T]he Department has implemented sanctions and procedures for addressing noncompliance. . . . and entities such as the BGA are not the proper organizations to undertake such an investigation."[107]

The decision is short of a clear recognition of Glomar response claims in Illinois. The decision was principally concerned with protecting the identity of individuals in the criminal database, and, curiously, the Glomar response is the method for doing so. This decision – perhaps more so than *Abdur-Rashid*, where the Glomar response was approved for NYPD use – signals cause for concern. Erratic or unreasoned implementation of the Glomar response threatens the purpose of the FOI system, potentially robbing exemptions of consistency and rationale. Further recognition in state and local courtrooms risks myriad applications and interpretations.

Procedure, Appeals and Review

The *Hashmi* opinion makes a strong case for the existing statutory scheme, particularly in utilizing the appeals process as outlined in the legislation.[108] That statutory procedure for FOIA was laid out in detail in the original 1966 legislation, but has seen a number of amendments calibrating its presumption of openness while protecting national security concerns. Those subject to FOIA include "any executive department, military department, Government corporation, Government

[104]Better Gov't Ass'n v. Zaruba, 21 N.E.3d 516, 518 (Ill. App. 2d 2014).

[105]*Id.* at 517-19.

[106]*Id.* at 527.

[107]*Id.*

[108]Hashmi v. N.Y. City Police Dep't, 998 N.Y.S.2d 596, 604 (2014) ("The adoption would effect a profound change to the statutory scheme that has been finely calibrated by the legislature. Therefore, the decision to adopt the Glomar doctrine is one better left to the state legislature, not to the judiciary.").

controlled corporation, or other establishment in the executive branch of the Government (including the Executive Office of the President), or any independent regulatory agency."[109] Each entity is responsible for making its records "available for public inspection and copying"[110] to "any person."[111] An individual must "reasonably describe" the records sought and comply with the minimal request standards of the agency.[112] There are also expectations of the agency regarding amount of time before initial response (twenty business days)[113] and what constitutes a satisfactory search of agency records.[114] There are nine exemptions that allow an agency to withhold disclosure of any responsive records.[115]

An individual unsatisfied with an agency response to a FOIA request may file an administrative appeal with the head of the agency.[116] The agency is expected to provide a determination on the appeal within twenty days.[117] A FOIA liaison assigned by each agency is responsible for overseeing the resolution of disputes.[118] Typically, a requester must exhaust the administrative appeals process before filing suit in the appropriate federal district court.[119] The D.C. Circuit Court has ruled the appeals process to be exhausted once an agency has issued a determination on a request.[120]

In appeals concerning exemption use or questions about nondisclosure, a district court will hear the case *de novo* and retains the ability to examine the records *in camera*.[121] The burden of proof in withholding responsive records lies with the agency, but "substantial weight" is to be given to defense affidavits.[122]

Two important review procedures have been implemented, one developed in common law and the other codified despite presidential objection. The two – Vaughn Indices and *in camera* review – are critical tools in checking overclassification.

[109] 5 U.S.C. § 552(f)(1) (2012).
[110] 5 U.S.C. § 552(a)(2) (2012).
[111] 5 U.S.C. § 552(a)(3)(A) (2012).
[112] *Id.*
[113] 5 U.S.C. § 552(a)(6)(A)(i) (2012).
[114] 5 U.S.C. § 552(a)(6)(E)(iii) (2012).
[115] 5 U.S.C. § 552(b) (2012).
[116] 5 U.S.C. § 552(a)(6)(A)(i) (2012).
[117] 5 U.S.C. § 552(a)(6)(A)(ii) (2012).
[118] 5 U.S.C. § 552(a)(6)(B)(ii) (2012).
[119] *See* Hidalgo v. FBI, 344 F.3d 1256, 1258 (D.C. Cir. 2003).
[120] Citizens for Responsibility & Ethics in Wash. v. FEC, 711 F.3d 180, 188 (D.C. Cir. 2012).
[121] 5 U.S.C. § 552(a)(4)(B) (2012).
[122] *Id.*

Prompted by the Watergate scandal and the controversial case *EPA v. Mink*,[123] Congress overrode President Gerald Ford's veto and passed amendments to the FOIA,[124] explicitly providing for *in camera* review of documents in appeals litigation.[125] Prior to the 1974 amendment, brief affidavits were enough to satisfy exemption from disclosure. In fact, the *Mink* decision expressly discouraged further scrutiny, forbidding *in camera* review Exemption 1 appeals and calling it beyond the purview of the statute.[126]

In *Vaughn v. Rosen*, the D.C. Circuit chose to comment directly on the deference of *Mink*, considering the court's role in determining exemption use.[127] Judge Malcolm Wilkey expressed concern in "assur[ing] a party's right to information is not submerged beneath governmental obfuscation and mischaracterization."[128]

In the original case, the court proposed the Vaughn Index as a method of judicial review with the judge calling for an itemized listing of records responsive to the FOIA request and individualized exemptions and justifications for each withheld record.[129] The court's stated objective for the Vaughn Index – "to make a rational decision [about] whether the withheld material must be produced without actually viewing the documents themselves . . . [and] to produce a record that will render [its]

[123] 410 U.S. 73 (1973).

[124] Privacy Act, Pub. L. 93-502, 88 Stat. 1561-1564; §§ 1-3 (1974).

[125] 5 U.S.C. § 552(a)(4)(B) (2012).

[126] 410 U.S. at 93.

[127] 484 F.2d 820, 824 (D.C. Cir. 1973) ("[T]he Supreme Court in *Mink* provided the outline of how trial courts should approach the job of making this factual determination. Our discussion here is intended to be an elaboration of this outline."). The Vaughn Index, established in *Vaughn v. Rosen*, 484 F.2d 820 (D.C. Cir. 1973), is an extension of the affidavit procedure, which asks an agency to provide the court with a justification of exemption claims. Vaughn Indices have become a common tool of judicial review whereby the withholding agency is asked to identify each non-disclosed portion of the sought records and justify withholding in each instance with an appropriate exemption. The practice requires federal agencies to be more exacting in their exemption use and allows courts to examine agency exemption use, particularly in cases involving a large volume of non-disclosed records).

[128] *Id.* at 826.

[129] *Id.* at 828 ("The current approach places the burden on the party seeking disclosure, in clear contravention of the statutory mandate. Our decision here may sharply stimulate what must be, in the final analysis, the simplest and most effective solution — for agencies voluntarily to disclose as much information as possible and to create internal procedures that will assure that disclosable information can be easily separated from that which is exempt. A sincere policy of maximum disclosure would truncate many of the disputes that are considered by this court. And if the remaining burden is mostly thrust on the Government, administrative ingenuity will be devoted to lightening the load.").

decision capable of meaningful review on appeal."[130] – demonstrated its efforts to provide sufficient review while respecting classification.

Ensuring the release of "reasonably segregable"[131] records is the primary purpose of a Vaughn Index. It is often used to spot check the verisimilitude of agency exemption use, with a sampling of exemptions and justification considered to determine the credibility of exemptions when voluminous records are under consideration.[132] In a 1991 case, a journalist chose approximately 2% of the responsive documents with the court ordering cited exemptions and explanations for each redaction or withheld document. The resulting Vaughn Index provided justifications for two-thirds of the sampled records while another third was reconsidered and determined to be available for release in full. Though the records released after the court-ordered Vaughn Index were viewed to not be symptoms of agency malfeasance or reason for bad faith, they did "persuade [the court] that it is incumbent upon the district court to examine closely the initial exemption claims."[133]

When Vaughn Indices are seen as unsatisfactory in providing enough detail, the Supreme Court has ruled that *in camera* review is an acceptable method of judicial review.[134] While the use of *in camera* examination of documents was amended to the FOIA, U.S. district courts retain "broad discretion"[135] in applying the remedy and do so only in exceptional cases.[136] Though not its central purpose, *in camera* review has been utilized in instances of bad faith.[137] In *Jones v. FBI*, the court turned to *in camera* scrutiny after finding "evidence of bad faith or illegality with regard to the underlying activities which generated the documents at issue."[138] Seen as particularly onerous, such review is disfavored.[139]

In camera review is most commonly used when affidavits explaining exemption justification are decided to be insufficient[140] or lacking

[130]King v. Dep't of Justice, 830 F.2d 210, 219 (D.C. Cir. 1987).

[131]5 U.S.C. § 552(b) (2012) ("Any reasonably segregable portion of a record shall be provided to any person requesting such record after deletion of the portions which are exempt under this subsection.").

[132]*See* Bonner v. Dep't of State, 928 F.2d 1148, 1151 (D.C. Cir. 1991) ("If the sample is well-chosen, a court can, with some confidence, 'extrapolate its conclusions from the representative sample to the larger group of withheld materials.'").

[133]*Id.* at 1152.

[134]Dep't of Justice v. Landano, 508 U.S. 165, 180 (1993).

[135]Loving v. Dep't of Defense, 550 F.3d 32, 41 (D.C. Cir. 2008).

[136]*See* Jones v. FBI, 41 F.3d 238, 243 (6th Cir. 1994).

[137]*See* Quiñon v. FBI, 86 F.3d 1222, 1228 (D.C. Cir. 1996).

[138]41 F.3d at 242-43.

[139]*See* Armstrong v. Executive Office of the President, 97 F.3d 575, 580-81 (D.C. Cir. 1996).

[140]*See* Rein v. U.S. Patent & Trademark Office, 55 F.3d 353, 377 (4th Cir. 2009).

in detail.[141] In *Quiñon v. FBI*, the D.C. Circuit took notice of affidavits that were merely declaratory and deficient in reasoning: "[W]here an agency's affidavits merely state in conclusory terms that documents are exempt from disclosure, an in camera review is necessary."[142] Notably, *in camera* inspection has been used when considering information claimed to already be in the public domain.[143]

Both Vaughn Indices and *in camera* review are critical elements of the FOIA appeals process. They afford the appellant an essential opportunity to question agency exemption use and allow the court to arbitrate federal non-disclosure efforts. The Glomar response, by withdrawing the necessary elements for such discourse, circumvents the appeals process in a manner beyond statutory consideration.

Official Acknowledgement and Waiver of Exemption Protection

As the efforts to acquire the mail covers records and the *Florez* case make apparent, appeals of a Glomar response can meet curious ends. In both instances, the records sought were in public circulation, yet the government would neither confirm nor deny their existence. Cases like these, where a widely documented federal program is essentially disavowed or the information on a diplomat three-decades removed from relevance, not only point to over-classification, and also demonstrate the extreme difficulty in overcoming a Glomar response. To challenge a Glomar response is to attempt to hit an invisible target. Instead of appealing the merits of disclosure, requesters are forced to demonstrate whether the public is already aware of potentially responsive records, a peculiar cause as the request itself is a type of public recognition. Two common law standards have emerged as methods for compelling disclosure when confronted with a Glomar response claim: official acknowledgement and waiver of exemption.

Federal courts have heard a number of cases considering waiver of exemption protection in non-Glomar FOIA appeals, where an exemption claim is deemed moot after the sought information was determined to have found its way into public discourse.[144] The D.C. Circuit has ruled that a plaintiff holds "the initial burden of pointing to specific

[141] *See* Spirko v. U.S. Postal Service, 147 F.3d 992, 997 (D.C. Cir. 1998).

[142] 86 F.3d at 1229.

[143] *See* Tigue v. Dep't of Justice, 312 F.3d 70, 82 (2d Cir. 2002); Mehl v. EPA, 797 F. Supp. 2d 43, 46 (D.D.C. 1992).

[144] *See, e.g.,* Assassination Archives & Research Ctr. v. CIA, 334 F.3d 55 (D.C. Cir. 2003); Frugone v. CIA, 169 F.3d 772 (D.C. Cir. 1999); Azmy v. Dep't of Defense, 562 F.

information in the public domain that appears to duplicate that being withheld."[145] Such an inversion of responsibility, with the requester required to provide justification for disclosure, is counter to the central premise of the FOIA. The threshold has also proved to be difficult to meet with ubiquitous press coverage often not compelling disclosure.[146] Demonstrating that requested information matches information that is already in public circulation has proved difficult, with one court stating the sought-after records must be equally as specific as the circulating information and also must be published by an "official and documented" source to be considered "officially acknowledged" and require disclosure.[147] Congressional reports[148] and a U.S. ambassador's testimony before Congress[149] failed to satisfy the official acknowledgement standard. The Second Circuit Court directly addressed official acknowledgment in *Wilner*, finding, "[A]n agency may invoke the Glomar doctrine to a FOIA request regarding a publically revealed matter. . . . [An agency] only loses its ability to provide a Glomar response when the existence or nonexistence of the particular records covered by the Glomar response has been officially or publically disclosed."[150]

Meeting the official acknowledgement threshold becomes more complicated when a FOIA request is given a Glomar response. It would seem simpler as "in the context of a Glomar response, the public domain exception is triggered when 'the prior disclosure establishes the existence (or not) of records responsive to the FOIA request,' regardless whether the contents of the records have been disclosed."[151] Demonstrating official acknowledgement of the existence of the sought records has proved a difficult mark to hit. Were an appellant to trigger official acknowledgement, it would only result in a non-Glomar response, opening the door to a traditional FOIA exemption appeal.

In an illustrative 2013 case, the D.C. Circuit Court overruled the CIA's use of a Glomar response when the American Civil Liberties Union sought agency information on drones.[152] The court recognized the use of the Glomar response in "limited circumstances," but only

Supp. 2d 590 (S.D.N.Y. 2008); Elec. Privacy Info. Ctr. v. Dep't of Justice, 584 F. Supp. 2d 65, 71 (D.D.C. 2008); Wheeler v. CIA, 271 F. Supp. 2d 132, 140 (D.D.C. 2003).

145 Afshar v. Dep't of State, 702 F.2d 1125, 1130 (D.C. Cir. 1983).

146 *See Azmy*, 562 F. Supp. 2d, at 598-99; Elec. Frontier Found. v. Dep't of Justice, 532 F. Supp. 2d 22, 24 (D.D.C. 2008).

147 Fitzgibbon v. CIA, 911 F.2d 755, 765 (D.C. Cir. 1990).

148 *Id.* at 765-66.

149 Pub. Citizen v. Dep't of State, 11 F.3d 198 (D.C. Cir. 1993).

150 592 F.3d 60, 70 (2nd Cir. 2009).

151 Marino v. DEA, 685 F.3d 1076, 1081 (D.C.Cir.2012) (quoting Wolf v. CIA, 473 F.3d 370, 379 (D.C. Cir. 2007)).

152 ACLU v. CIA, 710 F.3d 422 (D.C. Cir. 2013).

when the agency can demonstrate "harm cognizable under an FOIA exception."[153] Significantly, the court considered "official acknowledgement" in a FOIA appeal brought by the ACLU regarding CIA use of drones. In Chief Judge Merrick Garland's majority opinion, President Barack Obama and Chief of Homeland Security and Counterterrorism John Brennan's public addresses were cited as official acknowledgment of federal government interest in drone use. The court said non-avowal of a CIA intelligence interest in drone technology "strains credulity."[154] The specificity of Brennan's remarks along with then-CIA Director Leon Panetta publically asserting that remote drone strikes in Pakistan were "the only game in town" were seen as decisive in determining official acknowledgment.[155]

Judge Garland observed:

> The Glomar doctrine is in large measure a judicial construct, an interpretation of FOIA exemptions that flows from their purpose rather than their express language. In this case, the CIA asked the courts to stretch that doctrine too far — to give their imprimatur to a fiction of deniability that no reasonable person would regard as plausible.[156]

The D.C. Circuit remanded the case, ruling the Glomar response improper and asking the lower court to determine whether traditional denials under Exemption 1 and 3 claims were appropriate for nondisclosure.[157]

Legislative Proposals and Discussion

The 114th Congress considered the increased popularity of the Glomar response and the growing range of exemptions tethered to the reply and passed an amendment that would prohibit efforts to "withhold information requested. . . merely because disclosure of the information may be embarrassing to the agency or because of speculative or abstract concerns."[158] The Senate report on the possible changes explained an

[153] *Id.* at 426 (quoting Roth v. Dep't of Justice, 642 F.3d 1161, 1178 (D.C. Cir. 2011)).

[154] *Id.* at 430.

[155] Remarks of Leon Panetta, Director of CIA, at the Pacific Council on International Policy, May 18, 2009, *available at* https://www.cia.gov/news-information/speeches-testimony/directors-remarks-at-pacific-council.html.

[156] ACLU v. CIA, 710 F.3d, at 431.

[157] *Id.* at 434.

[158] FOIA Improvement Act of 2015, S. 337, 114th Cong.

agency may withhold information only if it reasonably foresees a *specific identifiable harm* to an interest protected by an exemption, or if disclosure is prohibited by law, commonly referred to as the "presumption of openness."[159]

The amendments look to address methods of abstraction like the Glomar response. Both in the letter and the spirit of the law, the post-submission discussion between the agency and requester is seen as critical in resolving concerns by either party. Twice in the FOIA statute, requester amenability is explicitly called for.[160] Obstinacy in working with the agency is noted as a consideration in the appeals process.[161] Often the requester will need to supply further specifications on what is being sought or the agency may steer the individual to the appropriate agency or department or better clarify the functions of the legislation.[162] Communication between individual and agency provides an important step in allowing the requester to better understand the FOIA system and the agency better able to serve the requester. This back-and-forth is an informal but important piece in achieving satisfactory ends.

It is hard to overstate the value of this discourse, as those most invested in the FOIA system understand the inherent give-and-take of the process. In the everyday gathering of records, stubbornness and hostility are uncommon paths and administrative appeals and federal court cases pursued as a last resort or as a grand gesture of disappointment with the system (as these rarely yield results). The Glomar response forecloses this vital element, and by extending this interplay, and not entirely dismissing it, the FOIA system as a whole is more likely to find agreeable ends for all parties involved. Neither confirming nor denying existence of the records moves the discourse outside of access to public records law, marking agency closure of the request. It is a denial, full stop; and exists as dead end to all avenues other than appeal and litigation. The Glomar response undermines access to public records in a number of ways, not least by obstructing civil efforts to work with the department or agency.

Another of the issues is an inherent failure of logic in the Glomar response, as identified by Nathan Freed Wessler:

[159] S. Rep. No. 114-4, at 8 (2015).

[160] 5 U.S.C. § 552(a)(6)(B)(ii) & 5 U.S.C. § 552(a)(6)(C)(iii) (2012).

[161] 5 U.S.C. § 552(a)(6)(B)(ii) (2012) ("Refusal by a person to reasonably modify the scope of a request or arrange an alternative time frame for processing a request (or a modified request) under clause (ii) after being given an opportunity to do so by the agency to whom the person made the request shall be considered as a factor.").

[162] 5 U.S.C. § 552(a)(6)(A)(I) (2012).

> Were the government to invoke the Glomar response only when it had responsive records that it wished to conceal, while giving a traditional "no records" when it had no such responsive records, then requestors would come to see the Glomar response as nothing more than a functional government admission that records existed but were being covered up.[163]

This becomes especially suspicious when there exists some public knowledge of the records being sought. Thus, the validity of the continued use of the Glomar response is contingent upon agency ability, not in utilizing the answer consistently, but in applying it with randomness (that is, to keep the public guessing). This surely is not an advisable path for federal governance.

As patterned use of the deflection method would invalidate it, the procedure rests on abdicating oversight. At present, the appeals system as facilitated in federal courts has provided the sustained deference necessary with few cases seeing substantial review.

While the Glomar response is problematic, it has a legitimate purpose in the FOIA scheme. To maintain its use, extending the request process (for example, as courts allow for extensive *voir dire* in court cases fraught with publicity concerns), particularly in refining requester language and expectations, may be an acceptable path forward. In allowing for communication and refinement of what is or is not potentially available, administrative appeals are apt to be more fruitful and could lead to fewer appeals in the federal court system. Hostile and contentious requests are legitimate regardless of tone, and agency reply should be systematic and oblivious to the voice of a request. The FOIA process, however, is a human process and acknowledgement of the interpersonal nature of the mechanism is necessary, and especially so when expanding discourse between requester and agency, an opportunity foreclosed upon with the Glomar response.

Danae Aitchison has called for further refinement of the FOIA, suggesting amending it in three ways: (1) Congress should require rare use of Glomar and only under limited circumstances; (2) Congress should provide courts with power to coerce compliance from agencies that fail to produce detailed, case-specific public affidavits; and (3) Congress should establish the review of *in camera* affidavits only as a last resort.[164] Implementing these changes would allow for the continued, responsible use of the Glomar response while allowing for a fuller public record.

[163]Nathan Freed Wessler, *[We] Can Neither Confirm Nor Deny the Existence of Nonexistence of Records Responsive to Your Request": Reforming the Glomar Response under FOIA*, 85 N.Y. U. L. Rev. 1381, 1396 (2010).

[164]Aitchison, *supra* note 52, at 251.

Contemporary national security concerns have shifted the powers of the tripartite federal government. In routinely deferring to agency national security claims, the court has effectively diminished its role and unbalanced the tuning of federal governance. By placing a thumb on the scale and allowing "substantial weight"[165] to agency affidavits so long as they hold "reasonably specific detail, demonstrate that the information withheld logically falls within the claimed exemption, and are not controverted by either contrary evidence in the record nor by evidence of agency bad faith."[166] When considering agency arguments, a court determines whether the position is "logical or plausible."[167]

As seen in the original Glomar Explorer mission, the official stance of ignorance only led to further suspicion and added fuel to the media spectacle. Civil liberty lawyers have taken advantage of the public backlash Glomar responses have often engendered. Jonathan Manes, previously of the ACLU and now Abrams Clinical Fellow at Yale's Information Society Project, cited Glomar responses as the first step in "transparency campaigns."[168] The FOIA denial is considered a catalyst or an anchor for advocacy. The thorough stonewalling of the Glomar response only increases citizen interest. Manes called the FOIA appeals process a platform for public attention, with each step another news peg.[169] Through the entirety of media events like NSA surveillance revelations, official government messaging is meticulously developed to avoid triggering FOIA obligations for further disclosure, allowing the state to shape public understanding with little accountability. The absurdity of asserting in court that secrecy is essential, while speaking about the issues in public (via official or unattributed channels) results in a dissonance that enflames public curiosity and rancor. The established exemptions and appeal process offer considerable latitude for classified information, especially so of national security concerns. In utilizing abstraction and obfuscation, agencies only provide oxygen for campaigns by civil liberties organizations.

The Department of Justice and the Office of Information Policy regularly create guides for federal agency reference in managing the FOIA. Since 1986, the section detailing use of the Glomar response has called

[165]Wilner v. NSA, 592 F.3d 60, 68 (2nd Cir. 2009).

[166]Larson v. Dep't of State, 565 F.3d 857, 862 (D.C. Cir. 2009).

[167]*Id.*

[168]Jonathan Manes, How National Security Information Flows to the Public: The Case of Targeted Killings, speech at the Rob Kling Center for Social Informatics Colloquium, Mar. 27, 2015.

[169]*Id.*

such a reply extraordinary and cautioned against utilization.[170] The increasing pervasiveness of the Glomar response and other evasive measures threaten the appeals process and the very heart of the FOIA itself. By heeding the OIP's early warning and returning to the statutory regime, a cornerstone of democracy will remain solid in providing the public its right to know.

Conclusion

A primary strength of the FOIA is its appeals process. Unlike many international access statutes, it provides an answerable independent federal court system, one finely calibrated by nearly five decades of hearing FOIA concerns. The Glomar response provides a loophole in this structure, undermining the very purpose of the law and its well-honed judicial review process. Expansion of the Glomar response threatens to unravel the fabric of access to government records. Its haphazard, illogical implementation would surely meet an equally quixotic judicial interpretation in the varied state and local courtrooms across the United States. While imperfect, the FOIA, and its many similar state and local statutes, help build a trust in government. Without a dependable method for acquiring the records necessary for ensuring accountable, transparent government, it would seem to follow that the threat of skepticism or even cynicism would metastasize.

The very existence of the Glomar response is not the problem. It serves a reasoned purpose in the present FOIA regime. This purpose, however, is to be narrowly defined and the reply utilized only in exceedingly rare instances where confirmation of records' existence poses a foreseeable harm to national security. Distributing this responsibility to states and smaller civic entities is inviting abuse of power. The familiar exemption structure that ably served FOIA for decades remains in place. A limited use of the Glomar response is acceptable, but to consent to recent efforts to expand use of the Glomar response into non-federal, non-national security concerns would be a grave mistake, one certain to send out ripples of discontent until rectified.

The primary issue with the Glomar response is its unreliable implementation among federal departments and agencies, and, as a result, it is frequently contested in federal court. Even among the landmark cases defining Glomar response use, there is little consensus. In affirming the Glomar response claim, the *Hunt* court expressed reticence in

[170] *OIP Guidance: Privacy "Glomarization,"* DEP'T OF JUSTICE, Jan. 1, 1986, http://www.justice.gov/oip/blog/foia-update-oip-guidance-privacy-glomarization.

the practice. In both *Wolf* and *ACLU v. NSA*, the courts found the agencies to have overreached.

The results of *North Jersey Media*, *Abdur-Rashid*, *Hashmi* and *BGA* are also mixed, but what the cases – and the Indiana amendment – represent is anything but ambiguous. They provide evidence of increasing implementation of the Glomar response. In the two New York cases, surveillance techniques were at stake. *North Jersey Media* presented an instance of the Glomar response as a shield for civilian privacy. The Illinois decision turned on the opening of a police database. *North Jersey Media* and *BGA* demonstrate the Glomar response at its most tenuous and unnecessary. Statutory exemptions would have sufficed in both situations, providing time-honored methods for non-disclosure. *Abdur-Rashid* and *Hashmi* only qualify for federally approved Glomar response under the premise that all Muslims are suspects. To affirm state-level Glomar response claims like these is to abandon oversight of surveillance programs broadly. The four state cases examined herein demonstrate the zealous and often dubious use of an extraordinary national security tool developed for extraordinary situations. A federally maintained Glomar response may have a time and a place, but utilization at the state and local levels is a bridge too far.

This study has traced the disconcerting recent expansion of Glomar response claims into non-federal, non-national security exemptions. While there exists a significant amount of research on the Glomar response (and nearly all of it critical of the practice[171]), none has documented the creep of the Glomar response into state statutes and courthouses. In documenting the surge of state interest, the study has explored the difficulty in appealing a Glomar response. Official acknowledgement and waiver of exemption are mercurial thresholds, difficult to satisfy. Challenging a Glomar response is an arduous task, and defeating a claim only places the requester back at the beginning of the labyrinth, appealing the exemption itself. State and local recognition of the Glomar response poses a serious threat to grassroots access both in multiplying the number of Glomar response claims and presenting a maze of court interpretations and rationales. It is imperative that the access community, and those who rely on readily available government information, remain alert to this threat, as expanded recognition and use threaten to turn the already trying access system into a dizzying funhouse of proving the very existence of records that cannot be seen.

[171] *See supra* note 23.

Index